Inside Stories: A Narrative Journey

Judy Robertson

Lisa Gjedde

Ruth Aylett

Rose Luckin

Paul Brna

Copyright © 2008 by Judy Robertson, Lisa Gjedde, Ruth Aylett, Rose Luckin and Paul Brna.

Published by NILE Press.

Illustrations by Maria Skov Pedersen

All rights reserved.

No part of this book may be reproduced in any form or by any electronic or mechanical means including information storage and retrieval systems, without permission in writing from the authors. The only exception is by a reviewer, who may quote short excerpts in a review.

Visit our website at www.narrativejourney.org

First Printing: November 2008
ISBN 978-0-9559817-0-8

Contents

Foreword	7
Acknowledgements	11
About the authors	13
Storytelling	17
Introduction	19
An urban legend	22
Storytelling in the classroom	26
What is a story?	27
The sea life project	30
Frame stories	33
Narrative structure	37
Types of stories	40
Of ants	43
Hidden messages	46
Modes of thought	48
Stories and culture	50
Multiple points of view	54
A game of Barnga	58

Storytelling in the curriculum	63
Sugar coated sea monsters	72
Princesses can be heroic too	80
Jo and Jerome discuss dyslexia	93
Not everyone likes stories	96
The ticket inspector	98
Jerome and Chris plan a study	101
Good night	108
Technology to support storytelling	**119**
Sugar rush	121
Is technology anti-social?	124
Making the invisible visible	127
Introducing Bugsy	132
Imaginary friends	138
Personalisation	141
Making games	144
Jerome is jumped by zombies	156
Filling in the gaps	161
How realistic should a game be?	164
The digital divide	168
At the fair	176

A Medieval Tale	178
Jerome as mermaid man	187
Fear of technology	195
Theatre in education	198
Simulation and drama	202
Violence in games	206
The advantages of unpredictability	210
Massively multiplayer online games	212
The wonderful world of blogging	223
The future of narrative learning	**231**
Jerome's dream	233
Jerome loses his bag	236
Journey end	248
Wikipedia	250
Physical interfaces	256
Goodbyes	265
Jerome's bag is returned	269
The Future of Narrative and Learning Technology	270
Index	**289**

Foreword

We invite you to come with us on a journey. As in all journeys, you will encounter new people and new points of view. The book is about a train journey during which our characters discuss questions about storytelling, learning and technology. They debate the ways in which storytelling can support learning, and explore technologies which can facilitate this. They don't always agree, but they nevertheless discuss their differing points of view, leaving you to make up your own mind. If you would like to know more about topics which the characters discuss, there are footnotes which direct you to further reading. You can also find additional material at www.narrativejourney.org.

This is a tale that is bound together by the authors out of a love of storytelling, a deep knowledge of current technologies and a conviction that, with care, technology can be used to support learning through storytelling. *Inside Stories* will lead you into the world of our research, where we aim to build technology that supports and values the individual learner. The book will succeed if you can see how to couple current technologies to support personal development through narrative in all its varied forms.

When we began the book, we wanted the form to match the content; we thought a volume about the value of storytelling should be in story form itself. You can judge the result for yourself, but writing it was certainly invigorating for us! We hope you will enjoy your own path through the book and find some information, insight or message that makes the effort worthwhile.

Acknowledgements

Storytellers like to say that whenever you tell a story, you stand on the shoulders of those who have told it before you. Likewise, we stand on the shoulders of all our friend and colleagues who have influenced our research. Together we have travelled through the landscapes of storytelling and technology, and we must thank them for making it such an inviting place to spend time. As we wrote the book, we started on a journey ourselves in the company of teachers and software developers, and lots of eager learners. We have found that the easiest sections to write are those which are based on real conversations with teachers and researchers. If you have chatted to any of us in the last two years about storytelling, technology or education, you may find parts of the conversation have found their way into this book. Although all of the characters are fictional, aspects of them have been inspired by real people. A lot of the projects described here are based on research projects we have carried out in schools with the generous support of teachers. In drawing on people we have met and experiences we have had, we hope to give the book a flavour of authenticity.

Our storytelling colleagues in the Scottish Storytelling Forum have given us a lot of ideas and advice over the years: they have taught us the value of storytelling.

This book would not have come about had it not been for the opportunities provided by the Engineering and Physical Sciences Research Council of the UK. It was the EPSRC who funded the first Narrative and Interactive Learning Environments (NILE) conference in 2000, and the second one in 2002. The Arts and

Humanities Research Council and the EPSRC also funded the "Drama and Performance for Pleasurable Personal Learning Environments (DAPPPLE)" project as part of an initiative connected with Culture and Creativity, and this funding also supported NILE 2006. The authors are particularly grateful to the EPSRC and the AHRC since the DAPPPLE project partly supported the work of writing this book.

Senga Munro gave us useful help and insight—as ever—on early drafts. Michael Young contributed greatly to the initial planning of the book. Maria Skov Pedersen amazed us with her ability to capture the heart of the stories in the book in her wonderful line drawings. Who else could draw a mermaid riding a winged horse with such style? Dominic Seymour patiently gave up his free time to help with designing the cover, drawing diagrams and proof editing. Fred Garnett also assisted with comments on the draft. Thank you, everyone.

About the authors

Judy Robertson[1] is a lecturer in Computer Science at Heriot-Watt University, where she works with Ruth Aylett. She is interested in working with learners and teachers to develop educational software. One of her current research projects explores how children can learn story writing skills through making their own computer games in the classroom. Judy is a member of the Scottish Storytelling Forum, and is a children's storyteller. She has published several academic papers on the topics of narrative, educational technology and learner-centred design.

Lisa Gjedde[2] is Associate Professor of ICT, Media and Learning at the School of Education, Aarhus University, Denmark. She has a background in communication studies, theatre and storytelling. Her research has for several years been aimed at exploring the learning potentials of story-based learning environments and narrative artifacts, and how the use of narrative may lead to engaging, inclusive and imaginative learning. Her recent work has been focused on the role of narrative in learning, the design of interactive and mobile learning environments, exploring tools for imaginative and creative learning and developing methods for exploring meaning making in interactive environments.

Ruth Aylett[3] is a Professor of Computer Science at Heriot-Watt University in Edinburgh where she leads the VIS&GE (Vision, Interactive Systems & Graphical Environments) research

---

[1] www.judyrobertson.typepad.com
[2] www.gjedde.net
[3] http://www.macs.hw.ac.uk/~ruth/

group. She coordinates the EU project eCIRCUS in which nine partners from the UK, Germany, Portugal and Italy are applying intelligent synthetic characters and emergent virtual drama to education against bullying. She researches interactive narrative and affective agent models and has an earlier background in AI planning and robotics, with more than 120 refereed publications to date.

Rose Luckin[4] is Professor of Learner Centred Design at the London Knowledge Lab, a Visiting Professor at the Ideas Lab at the University of Sussex and an EPSRC Advanced Research Fellow. The aim of her research is to better understand the process of learning with technology and to use this to design technology effectively, to stimulate curiosity, maintain engagement and foster creativity. She is particularly interested in the development of participatory methods to engage learners and teachers in the process of designing technology to fit their needs. Her recent work has considered the role of context and the ways in which an increased understanding of the nature educational contexts might enable us to better support learning with pervasive and ubiquitous technologies.

Paul Brna[5] has been working in the area of learning environments for nearly 30 years. He has worked as a mathematics teacher, a university lecturer, and an educational consultant. He was the Director of the Computer-based Learning Unit at Leeds University, and more recently, became the Director of the SCRE Centre, an organisation that has carried out

---

[4] http://www.lkl.ac.uk/cms/index.php?option=com_comprofiler&task=userProfile&user=128
[5] http://web.mac.com/paulbrna

educational research in Scotland for 80 years. His research interests are in issues connected with Narrative and Interactive Learning Environments and include work on emotion and empathy in learning. He has organised the Narrative and Interactive Learning Environments (NILE) series of conferences and was coordinator of the Drama and Performance for Pleasurable Personal Learning Environments (DAPPPLE) research network.

Storytelling

Introduction

The new Trans-Europe Express stood sleekly gleaming in the station. From Atlantic to Pacific in four days: it was the product of the biggest international collaborative transport project ever conceived. Inside, each carriage included sets of four bedrooms each with a small living area attached where travellers could sit during the day and watch the scenery. The living area for carriage six lay empty, expectant, waiting for intrepid travellers who would rather take their time and spare the planet.

The door opened. A tall man entered, not in his first youth, smartly dressed in a well-cut grey suit and subtly striped shirt with a jaunty silk bow-tie. He had neatly brushed white hair and beard, and an even tan, with a smart black leather bag under his arm. He sat down in the living area, took a newspaper out from his bag and began to read.

The door opened again. This time a woman entered. She was fairly young – late twenties maybe, small, slender but very determined-looking. The man looked up. She had short, very blond hair, in spikes. She wore practical travel trousers with pockets down the legs and a navy body-warmer with pockets all down the front. She carried a large red rucksack with pockets all over it. "What does she have in all those pockets?" wondered the man. He put his paper down and smiled.

"Hello," he said. "It seems likely that we are going to share this living area for quite a long journey. I hope you won't mind if I introduce myself?" He sounded well-educated and courteous.

The woman glanced at him sharply, as if looking for an ulterior motive. He smiled back politely. She shrugged.

"Jerome Fletcher. I'm off to the UNESCO Future of Learning Festival – I work at the Learning Theory Centre in Brussels," he said.

The woman smiled. "Bit of a coincidence then. I'm going there too. Ada Greenwood. I'm a computer scientist though, a techie you might say. Going to show them some of the cool stuff that's around now. I'm at the Creative Futures Lab in Paris." She put her rucksack down, and took an mp3 player out of one of its pockets.

Jerome looked thoughtful, or maybe even a little intimidated. He felt the world already had too many gadgets. But before he could say anything, the door opened again. Another woman came in. She was a little older than Ada and taller. She had loosely permed brown hair, and was wearing a dark trouser suit with a neat cotton blouse. She had a brooch in the shape of a small green dragon on her lapel. Ada and Jerome both smiled at her.

"Oh, hello! Is this coach six?" She had a strong Welsh accent. "I'm Chris Headington. Isn't this exciting? All the way across two continents! I'm going to a Future of Learning Festival – how about you two?"

"So am I," Ada and Jerome said simultaneously, and then laughed.

"That's good—we'll be together all the way then. I've been chosen by my education authority to represent all the schools in my area at the festival—it's such an honour. I teach Year Fours. How about you?"

Ada and Jerome introduced themselves, and they all sat down together.

"So we must have three of the four bedrooms," Ada said. "Do you think there's someone in the fourth?"

Introduction

As she said this, the door opened again, but this time three people came in at once: a harassed looking man with two children, a boy just moving from child to adult, large and a little clumsy in his movements, and a small girl fizzing with excitement.

"Jo, Alex, get a move on!" he told the children in a stressed tone. "I have to get off before the train starts."

He saw Chris and a look of relief swept across his face. "Miss Headington! Here we are at last."

Chris got up at once. "Nice to see you again, Mr Warner. Hello Alex, you must really be looking forward to this big adventure."

The small girl rushed up. "Miss, Miss, we're going all the way from one sea to the other!"

Chris turned to Ada and Jerome. "This is Alex Warner—she's from my class. She's part of the learners' delegation—the rest of them are further down the train. She's the youngest pupil on the trip. How old are you now Alex?"

"I'm eight. I had my birthday last week."

"And this is Alex's brother Jo," Chris added, turning to the boy. "Jo, you and I will have to make sure we look after Alex. I'm relying on you, you know."

Jo looked as if he felt this might not be altogether fun. "OK," he muttered. "Bit of a tall order keeping Alex under control sometimes, but I'll try."

Alex squawked and prodded him in the stomach.

"Miss, don't let him push me around will you?"

Her father adopted a stern manner. "Alex, you know we expect you to behave. You've been picked from all the schools in our area, don't let us down. Jo, you have my authority to tell Alex what to do—Alex, is that clear?"

Alex looked down glumly. Jo nodded responsibly.

"Right kids, I have to get off." He kissed Alex, and hugged Jo. He left, and the two children stood there looking a bit uncertain.

"Come and sit down," Chris told them in a professionally cheerful manner. "This is Jerome and Ada, I'm sure you'll like them."

The kids sat down. A whistle blew. The outside doors clicked to locked.

Alex squawked again, pointing at the window. "Look! Look! We're moving!"

The journey had begun.

An urban legend

Chris settled herself back in her seat, pleased that the journey was underway. She knew that Alex would be content for hours yet, engrossed in her volume of *Stories from around the World*. She was curled up in the corner of the carriage, her juice forgotten, as she eagerly turned the pages. Jo, on the other hand, was obviously not so happy. She was just remembering that Jo's teacher mentioned that he was dyslexic and prone to frustration, when Jo threw the book on to the table with enough force to knock over Alex's juice, narrowly missing Ada's laptop. "*Stupid* book!"

"Honestly," he huffed. "Why do I have to read this stuff for school? I'd rather see the film. What good is it to me?" He slumped into his hooded top, a picture of sullenness.

An urban legend

As she helped Alex mop up the spill, Chris chatted to Jo. Luckily Ada had gone to sleep almost as soon as she had sat down and hadn't noticed. To distract Jo from his sulk, she told him about something her neighbour told her just before she left:

"It happened to a friend of hers. She bought a yucca plant and put it in her living room. It was all fine until one day she noticed there was a humming noise coming from the plant pot. 'How odd,' she thought to herself. But the noise just kept getting louder and louder until eventually she decided to call the garden centre. She thought they would just laugh at her, but they said 'Hold on, madam. Don't touch it or go near it, and we'll be round immediately.' Sure enough, half an hour later someone from the garden centre arrived. When he heard the humming sound he blanched and rushed the plant outside onto the back grass as fast as he could, just as the base of the stalk burst open! And there was this huge, hairy spider inside – a tarantula![6]*"*

Jo looked impressed in spite of himself.

"Ewww," said Alex, drawn out from her fairy tale.

"But the worst part is that the garden centre guy explained that those spiders only make that humming noise when they're ready to mate, and they only do it when there's a mate close by. So they reckoned that somewhere in that house there must be another tarantula!"

"*Cool*," said Jo.

"It's a good urban legend, that one," remarked Jerome, peering over his rimless spectacles. "One of my favourites."

---

[6] This urban legend is a variant of the Spider in the Yucca legend. Brunvand, J. H. (1993). The baby train and other lusty urban legends. New York ; London, W.W. Norton.

Inside Stories: A Narrative Journey

"What's an urban legend?"

"It's a sort of story which you hear going round about some remarkable or unexpected event to do with modern day life. Usually you hear about it happening to a friend of a friend, but never to someone you actually know. And then it turns out that the same story crops up all over the country, or sometimes all over the world, maybe over a period of years. The interesting thing about it is that there must be some fascination in the stories. They must really strike a chord with people to be passed from person to person like that. It is as if they have a life of their own."

"Lots of stories seem to strike a chord with my pupils," commented Chris thoughtfully. "I can never quite predict what a story will mean to the children, and it's different from child to child. Sometimes the same child will come across a story again a year later and they get something completely different out of it. I suppose there's growing room in stories."

"The same is true for folk tales," continued Jerome, warming to his theme. "The same stories crop up across cultures. There are thousands of versions of Cinderella, for example. The first recorded version is Greco-Egyptian from around the first century BC[7]. For that story to survive, it must resonate with people. The message is still as meaningful to people now as it ever was."

"Oh but some of those folk stories are so violent," objected Chris. "They're just full of dreadful things like people getting eaten and parents killing children and so on."

---

[7] Wikipedia, c. (28 May 2008 20:06 UTC). "Cinderella." Retrieved 29 May 2008 16:04 UTC, from
http://en.wikipedia.org/w/index.php?title=Cinderella&oldid=215571805.

An urban legend

"There's a story in my book like that from Japan," Alex said. "It's about a lady who gets made into soup by a badger, and then her husband nearly eats the soup! It's horrid!" [8]

Jo perked up some more. "Yeah," he said. "Those are great. Because you think it's going to be some stupid kids' story but then it turns out to be really dark. I like that."

"Bruno Bettelheim [9] would agree with you there, young man," Jerome said. "He argues that children have a need to explore the darker themes in stories in a safe environment and it is a way to work through the fears which fascinate us. More recently, Gerard Jones [10] has made a similar argument about violent themes in comic books, TV and computer games. He points out that there is a difference between play fighting after watching TV cartoons, and actually fighting. His argument is that it's important to act out the violence to explore it and lessen its impact. Encountering violence in stories doesn't mean you will be violent in real life."

"Well doh!" said Jo, not much impressed by this explanation from well known theorists. "Any kid could tell you that."

"Hey! Alex," he said after a pause. "Someone at school told me this story about how their friend was out driving at night and she broke down. She turned on her radio and there was this news report about a madman escaped from a prison. And her boyfriend went to get help and when he was gone she heard this *scraaatching* sound along the car roof and then there was blood trickling..."

---

[8] *The Farmer and the Badger*. Ozaki, Y. T. The Japanese fairy book. Compiled by Yei Theodora Ozaki, Rutland.
[9] Bettelheim, B. (1976). The uses of enchantment : the meaning and importance of fairy tales. London, Thames and Hudson.
[10] Jones, G. (2002). Killing monsters : why children need fantasy, superheroes, and make-believe violence. New York, BasicBooks ; Plymouth : Plymbridge.

"Ahem… Alex—would you like another biscuit?" Chris interjected loudly, feeling Jerome's theories might be all very well but she had no wish to stay up all night with a scared 8 year old suffering from night terrors.

Storytelling in the classroom

"I did enjoy your story there," said Jerome to Chris a little later. "You told it very well."

"Oh well, I do enjoy telling stories in the class. I always have done. My Gran used to tell me stories when I was little so I like to pass them on to the class. Some of them just don't get stories otherwise and it's so important for children, I feel. Some of the children's parents read to them a lot, or else their grandparents do, but then there are others who only seem to know stories if they've been in films. I think parent have less time for reading and it's a real shame. I can understand it of course—everyone is so busy these days—but I wouldn't want the kids to lose out. Stories are so valuable. So every day I make a space for story time. We gather round in a corner of the class and they settle down and I tell them a story."

"That's marvellous," Jerome said admiringly. "How wonderful to have that talent! I'm sure the children love your storytelling. It's quite different from reading stories though, isn't it?"

"It is, although I do read out loud sometimes too. But I prefer storytelling because it's more …well… more *personal* somehow.

More intimate. I really feel a strong connection with the class when I tell a story because I have eye contact all the time. I can see how it affects my children—who's enjoying it, who's puzzled, if I've hit a nerve. I can change the story a little bit when I want to, to include ideas they have. Or if they look bored I can liven it up, or if they look too scared—bless them!—I can make it more funny."

"Of course teachers are good at diagnosing their classes' learning during normal teaching," commented Jerome.

"Yes, of course they are! This is different in a way, though. I think it lets me get to know my children as people more. Once we had a visiting storyteller (just superb!) and she said that stories were about the whole child. I think she meant that stories are as much about emotional learning as they are about literacy development and so on."

"Hmmm... I can see that," Jerome mused. "I suppose they can empathise with the characters, and identify with their struggles."

What is a story?

"But where do you get all your stories from?" Jo asked curiously.

"Well, I've heard a lot of stories," said Chris. "Some are from books, and some just come to me."

"It's odd," said Jerome slowly. "Stories seem so basic. One can imagine early humans sitting round a fire in a cave telling them. Half our memories seem to be made of stories about things that have happened to us. Yet I'm not sure we really know what a story is."

Chris looked surprised. "Well, stories have a beginning, a middle and an end. They have characters. And things happen to them—they have adventures, they fight dragons. Or spiders," she laughed.

"But computer games have lots of characters killing things," Jo objected. "I like the blood and gore but they don't feel like stories to me. Even the role-playing ones I've played don't really. They're more about finding the key to the treasure chest or how to get into the control room."

"There is a difference between problem-solving and a story," Jerome replied. "We know it and we feel it, but it's hard to explain why. I think perhaps it has to do with emotion."

"It is frustrating when you can't get into the control room," Jo responded.

"But think about Chris' yucca story," Jerome said. "The characters interact and their emotions change."

"All that happens when I do online chat with my friends," Jo objected. "But that doesn't feel like a story either."

"But that's because you're just chatting," Chris said. "No dragons get killed. And in your blood-thirsty games, it's all killing and no chat."

"So it seems that both changes in the real world and interaction between characters is needed to make a set of events into a story," Jerome said. "And there has to be some kind of causal chain between them."

Chris and Jo looked at him, confused.

What is a story?

"Oh, maybe I haven't explained that very clearly, have I?" said Jerome. "I know, let me draw a picture."

He pulled out a serviette from the metal box on the table they were sitting round, helpfully provided for use at mealtimes. Then he removed a smart gold-capped pen from the top pocket of his jacket and drew on the serviette. It looked like a figure-of-eight lying on its side.

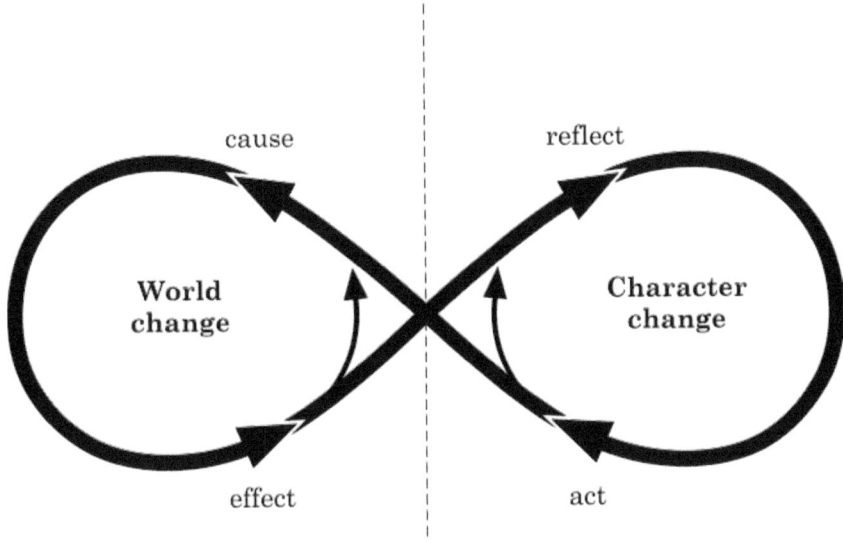

The causal chain of a story

"Think of it as a process," Jerome said, moving his pen around the figure-of-eight. "Look, at this end there's some change in a character—some motive, some emotion, some goal. That causes things in the world to change. For example the hero kills the dragon because he wants to marry the princess. Then that change in the world causes changes in the character—he marries the princess and his goal is fulfilled."

"But don't forget the beginning, the middle and the end," said Chris. "Otherwise almost any bit of real life could be a story. We could be in a story."

"You're right of course," Jerome said. He drew a box around the figure-of-eight. "This is the story-world. This is how it is at the start—he drew a thick line on the left-hand edge of the box. "And this is how it is at the end when the prince has married the princess." He drew a thick line on the right-hand edge.

"So why does the prince never have to go to the bathroom?" asked Jo.

Jerome thought for a moment. "Well, it doesn't fit into a causal chain really. It neither changes the prince's emotions nor does it change anything significant in the world." He laughed. "Although I suppose if the prince had been in the bathroom when the dragon attacked the castle and therefore not able to kill it, then it would have got a mention."

The sea life project

Chris was looking through the materials her class were going to display at the conference.

"Isn't this lovely?" she asked "I'm so proud of the children."

She showed the others a collage which her class had made for the exhibition. The class had been working on stories of the sea, so all the children had contributed drawings and paintings of sea creatures, mythical and real, in beautiful shades of blue and green.

The sea life project

Jerome looked appreciatively at the artwork. "Which age-group did you say did this?"

"My Year 4 class—around 8 year olds."

Alex pointed at a figure in the collage. "Look, this is my mermaid."

"Isn't that rubbish? Don't you ever learn anything proper?" said Jo with a tone only a brother can muster.

Chris looked at Jo reprovingly. "Now, now, Jo!"

"It's very nice," said Jerome kindly.

"But I *did* learn lots of things. I learned how to use pastel pencils and a lady came and showed us how to do cut outs. Then we did a story about it. I learned about mermaids. And crabs."

Jerome smiled and nodded along. She paused.

"And I learned to think [11]."

Jerome choked on his tea. "To think?" he asked in surprise.

Chris looked slightly smug. She was beginning to like it when she could surprise Jerome.

"Mermaids?" snorted Jo. "There are no mermaids."

"We learned about sharks too. I bet you didn't know that some types of sharks die if they stop swimming, smarty pants!"

"I knew that," said Jo, resolving to look this up on *Wikipedia* when he got home.

Jerome said to Chris "Can you explain a bit more about the project?"

"Well, we did it as a project based on a story-line. I started with telling them a story about an old woman who adopted a mermaid daughter. And then we decided to explore life in the sea.

---

[11] This is an actual quote from a child involved in a digital storytelling and animation project in Denmark.

We went on a field trip to the sea-life centre and collected sea-shells from the beach."

"We got to feed the sharks!"

"A pity they didn't eat you," muttered Jo.

"And then we went home to the library," said Alex, ignoring this, "and we found all the stories about mermaids we could. And there were lots and lots of them. I found a Welsh story about a mermaid who married a man and they both went to live in the sea. My friend Alice found one where the mermaid could go home to the sea but her husband couldn't, and that was really sad. We all wrote own stories too."

Chris tried to get a word in "We wrote a play together."

"And I played the cod fish!" shouted Alex, bouncing up and rushing around the carriage opening her mouth to blow bubbles like a fish. Jo rolled his eyes.

Chris smiled. "As you can see, the kids were really excited. I've never seen them work so hard. They even came in at lunchtime because they were so keen to work on their stories. Even kids who used to struggle with writing found they could be part of it, because they could be in the play, or add to the collage or help to make up the stories. There was one child who had never been able to write down his ideas, so I assumed he didn't have any at all. And then I was so pleased when he turned out to have a fantastic imagination and he came up with such a wonderful story. I felt a bit bad because I had kind of given up on him but all I needed to do was give him a new way to succeed. It really built his confidence. You should have seen his face when friends liked his ideas. His mum came to the play performance at the end of term and she was so proud of him because he was the star of the show. You wouldn't know he's the same boy now.[12]"

Jerome was surprised by that, but being Jerome he had to find out more "Are you saying then, that the children all worked on the same story?"

"Yes," Chris confirmed. "You see, this is what kept the class going on the same note. All the children first heard the same story, then did some exploration on a subject they wanted to know more about, then developed individual stories and worked together on making a play where they could use all their ideas."

"You mean, you let the children choose the subject they were to work on?"

"Yes of course," Chris answered, "but I picked the first story and the theme to match the curriculum content I had to cover."

"This sounds like a type of frame-story."

Frame stories

"What exactly do you mean by a frame-story?"

"A frame-story is a meta-narrative," began Jerome, settling back in his seat with his hands clasped across his waistcoat, "which provides a skeleton for other stories, like a Russian doll."

---

[12] All examples like this have been developed based on children we've met during research projects.

"Russian dolls don't have skeletons! Well, mine doesn't. It's empty inside apart from all the little dolls. There are 6 dolls and they're all red and blue."

Chris quelled Alex with a glance. She had a feeling that Jerome's undergraduate students wouldn't have dared to comment during such a speech.

"I'm sure you all know *Arabian Nights* or *Canterbury Tales* or *The Decameron*."

"I don't," said Jo.

Alex piped up again "I know about Arabian Nights. It was a King who had lots of wives and every night he killed one of them. One day it was the turn of a lady called Scherezad, but she was so clever that to save her life, she told him such an interesting story that it took all night and she hadn't even finished it by the morning. So he had to let her live, because he really wanted to know what happened next. The next night she told him the rest of that story, and started another one, and she kept on doing that and it ended up that he fell in love with her because she was so good at telling stories. And they lived happily ever after."

"Thank you, Alex," said Jerome. "You see, that way of putting a story inside other stories helps to keep the reader interested and to have a unifying overarching story which integrates different perspectives and builds a consistent universe."

Chris said "I didn't have lots of stories embedded in one big story. It was more like we used the setting and the theme of the sea from the initial story I told them. The initial story was like planting several seeds, and the children's own stories grew from them."

Frame stories

Jerome replied "Yes, I agree that is slightly different from Arabian Nights, where the stories are told sequentially within one story. That is more common within a literary framework, but your way of framing a project with a story also sounds very effective. Of course some people may argue it would increase the cognitive load of the listener to maintain track of the nested stories. On the other hand one may reply that it can be very helpful in maintaining a shared story-world within a class over a longer period."

"Boring," said Alex and rushed out into the corridor.

"I found that interesting," said Jo. "What does cognitive load mean?"

"Don't go there, Jo," Chris advised, eager to avoid another lecture.

"Cognition is to do with knowing. With thought. Cognitive load means that your mind has a lot to think about at the same time. It's like a cage full of monkeys that start jumping up and down at the same time."

"That sounds familiar," said Chris, dryly.

"And you can't concentrate on what one monkey is doing because all the others are distracting you! If you put more monkeys in the cage it becomes even more difficult to focus on what the single monkey is doing. It's like when you try to think on one more thing, when you've already got a lot on your mind."

Jo looked thoughtful. It was starting to make sense to him why he found reading so difficult.

Chris said "How come then, that stories that are very complex or complicated sometimes go down so well with kids that can't sit still otherwise? I've seen this so often."

Jerome replied "Actually these two things don't exclude each other. When we look at how cognition functions with stories—and this is a big area, mind you—then there are several reasons. As you know stories have a special structure. That has been recognized going back to the Greeks."

"You mean: beginning, middle, and end?" interrupted Chris.

Jerome nodded "Exactly, Aristotle in his *Poetics*. But since Aristotle there have been other theories that elaborate on the original structure and seek to understand the workings of the human mind, through making models of narrative processing and comprehension. Narrative is understood to be the original and fundamental way of knowing about yourself and the world."

"But how can you know about it, if it is going on inside other people's minds?" Jo wanted to know. "I saw something on television of people having their brains x-rayed."

"No, not brain-imaging in this case, but other techniques that psychologists use for getting to know how people perceive themselves and the world. For instance a psycho-linguist called Labov did a study of the way teenagers told stories in the inner city of New York.[13] The researcher asked them to talk about a time when they had been in danger. He found that their oral stories had a similar structure to each other, and other psychologists have found the same structure in different groups of people, even in very young children."

"Well, what are they?" asked Jo and Chris at the same time.

---

[13] Labov, J. a. W., W. (1997). "Narrative Analysis: Oral Versions of Personal Experience." Journal of Narrative and Life History 7(1-4): 3-39.

Narrative structure

"What they would consider a well-formed story would consist of six parts: a *resume* which sums up what the story is about; an *introduction* which identifies place, time and characters..."

Chris understood. "Ah, so the resume would be when I tell the class: 'I'm going to tell you a story about an old lady who gets a mermaid for a daughter'. And then I normally say a bit about how the old lady was lonely and how she lived by the sea a long time ago. That's the introduction."

Jerome nodded. "And then comes the development of the *core action* of what happens in the story."

"Like when the old lady finds the mermaid washed ashore in a clamshell and decides to take care of her, and so on..."

Jerome asked: "Do you usually make it clear why you are telling that story to the class? That would be the structural element called *evaluation*, which makes it clear why you are telling just that particular story, to that particular audience."

"Do you mean explaining the moral of the story?" asked Chris.

"It could be, but it need not be explicit. It can also reflect on the personal meaning the story has for the teller. In oral everyday storytelling or anecdotes the teller often uses the story to portray a positive image of himself. That's what Labov found with those New York teenagers."

"With fairy tales I often ask the class to tell me the point of the story after it is finished," commented Chris.

"During the core action a problem is usually raised, to which of course, characters must find a *solution*: this is the fifth structural element."

Chris pointed out "Of course the solution may not be a happy one, though that is what my kids prefer."

"And then the storytelling session finishes with what is called a *coda* which signals that the story is at an end and we return to normal conversation."

"Is the structure the same for all types of stories?" wondered Chris.

"Well, this particular model is, as I said, based on oral storytelling. As you can see it is not necessarily a linear model. This means that parts don't always happen in the same order."

"But what does all that have to do with my question about why kids enjoy complex stories?" Chris felt that Jerome had an inclination to wander off the point.

"Life is complex isn't it? And stories reflect life, so the kids enjoy both the parts that they immediately can understand as well as the parts that are more difficult for them to grasp. In a way you can say that when they listen to a story they build on the understandings that they already have, and can develop new understanding from that point."

Chris thought about this. "Are you saying that because the story follows a pattern (those six stages you told us about) that it helps the kids to make sense of the hard bits? I mean, following a structure simplifies parts of the story, leaving more space in their heads for understanding the tricky bits. The moral conundrums, or the complicated feelings. A bit like all those monkeys you mentioned. The patterns which they know about have the effect of quietening down some of the monkeys, and then they have more time to concentrate on the new monkeys. Is that what you mean?"

Jerome pondered "Yes, you may say that the use of a known story structure can help put the monkeys at ease, so to speak, so it becomes easier to understand the causal connections and relations and to acquire the knowledge. You will have perhaps observed that children often like to hear the same story repeated over and over again. They are learning about the structure as well as the content of the story. But when they are a bit older they can then predict the outcome of the story if it follows the classical pattern. They can find this boring. Some older children prefer the suspense it generates to have stories embedded in other stories, so the pattern is not so obvious."

This reminded Chris of her own experience. "I see what you mean. I taught a Year One class a few years ago and they just loved to hear about Goldilocks and the Three Bears every day. I got fed up telling them because once Goldilocks has tried the first version of the chair or the bed or the porridge you just know what is going to happen next! And you have to go through it all another two times for the mummy bear and the baby bear. So tedious."

Jerome laughed in acknowledgment. "Even though it may feel tedious to an adult, it is nevertheless a very important part of children's development to learn by repetition of the story. It gives the child a good start for developing their own narrative competences. This mastery of the simple form is what makes the more complex form absorbing for the child. A child that masters narrative expression will find it easier to communicate with others and to have empathy with them. So much of children's play consists of building imaginary worlds which is based on an understanding of causal structure and consistent character roles."

"I used to get really irritated with Alex when she was little, because she always wanted to make Darth Vader good instead of bad," Jo jumped in.

"Her interpretation of this story may not have been consistent with the film version of the story, but if she always played Darth Vader as a good character she had her own logic."

Alex ran back into the carriage. "Guess what I saw?"

"Monkeys in cages?" asked Jo.

Alex looked at him scornfully "No, we just passed a field of white horses." She settled down with her sketching pad and started to draw.

"What's that?"

"A horse, dumbo!"

"Dumbo was an elephant not a horse," replied her brother.

Types of stories

Chris had spotted Jerome's copy of *The Great Fairy Tale Tradition*[14] and asked politely if she could have a look at it. Flicking through the contents page she saw chapters on: *Bloodthirsty Husbands, The Fate of Spinning, Shrewd Cats,*

---

[14] Zipes, J. D. (2001). <u>The Great fairy tale tradition : from Straparola and Basile to the Brothers Grimm : texts, criticism.</u> New York, W.W. Norton.

Types of stories

Virtuous Queens and even *Incestuous Fathers*. She wondered why incestuous fathers (page 26) seemed to be more prominent than the other categories. One might have thought that inconvenient marriages would be more common, and yet they didn't appear until page 717. "This is an interesting book," she said raising an eyebrow.

Jerome said enthusiastically "Yes, isn't it great? It sheds light on the Brothers Grimm and how they collected their stories. Many people believe that the Brothers simply collected the tales from simple folktales orally passed down through generations of country folk, but it turns out they also made literary contributions to the tales themselves."

"Their stories are still well known today," commented Chris, "Snow White, Hansel and Gretel, Rapunzel and so on. Have you studied a lot about the different types of stories and where they came from, then?"

"I believe that it is difficult to separate content and form, but sometimes it can be helpful to be able to classify stories, and to clarify their purpose and origins. Personally I find it helpful to separate stories into the categories of folktales and myths."

"What's the difference between a folktale and fairytale?" Jo asked thickly, through a mouthful of Jaffa cakes.

"Fairytales are a type of folktale, usually containing magic and supernatural going-ons. Actually there are other types of folktales as well, like animal-tales which come in three different types: the etiological, the moral fable and the beast epic"[15].

---

[15] See the 'folktale' entry in: Columbia University. (2004). The Columbia encyclopedia. New York, Columbia University Press: xiv, 3156 p.

Inside Stories: A Narrative Journey

Jo spluttered crumbs. "Beast epic? Eti-what? Are you having me on or have you swallowed the dictionary for breakfast, Jerome?"

"Jo! Do mind your manners!" admonished Chris.

"I'm sorry," said Jerome contritely, "I tend to forget I'm not lecturing a class. Etiological stories are stories about origins. They explain why things are the way they are today."

"I tell my class a story about how the elephant got its long trunk. There are lots of stories like that. How the bear lost his tail, that kind of thing." Chris said.

"Whereas a beast epic is a satirical story about animals which comments on human society. A modern example would be Animal Farm by George Orwell." Jerome replied.

Jo groaned. "We had to read that at school."

Alex said "I like horses better than pigs." She was playing with her cuddly horse, making it gallop across the tabletop.

"That's a nice horsy," said Jerome, making an effort not to lecture, "what's its name?"

"She's called Peggy," said Alex, "Look—she's even got wings."

Jerome laughed "Peggy for Pegasus?" he asked.

Alex looked bewildered. "What's Pegasus?"

"Well, that brings us to the Myths category. Myths are stories about gods, heroes and other fantastic creatures. Pegasus is a winged horse in Greek mythology. He was muse to the poets."

"Big deal," muttered Jo under his breath.

"He also carried the thunderbolts for Zeus, the king of the gods and god of sky and thunder."

"That's more like it!" said Jo.

Alex added a thunderbolt to her drawing of the horse. Jerome went on, "Pegasus was actually ridden by Eos the goddess of Dawn. Why don't you put that in your picture Alex?" he said encouraging.

Alex reached for her yellow pen. "Stories are cool," she said happily.

Of ants

Alex had finished with her drawing for the time being. Now she was watching a film on Jo's games console. Jerome observed her for a little while. Obviously he wasn't familiar with such devices.

He interrupted Alex with a question. "That's a special thing you've got there. What is it you are watching?"

Alex barely glanced at him. "It's Jo's PSP. He only lets me borrow it sometimes. I like to watch films on it. I got *A Bug's Life* for my birthday so that's what I'm watching. It's got special features too."

Jerome looked puzzled "Special features? What would they be?"

"Oh, you always get those with films now. It's extra bits about the film and games and things. In this one it shows all the little ant families in their houses[16]. But I always like to watch the film first and then go to the special features." Alex turned back to her film, not wanting to be distracted further by what she thought were silly questions.

Jerome turned to Chris. "This is so different from when I was child. As you say, stories were what we had for entertainment, in

---

[16] It doesn't, actually. We're just using it to make a point.

my young day. My granddad had a book with stories that I loved to hear. He wasn't a storyteller but I quickly learned to read them to myself. And one of those that I liked most was about ants."

Chris asked "Which story do you mean?"

Jerome said "The story about the grasshopper and the ant. I've read it so many times I know it by heart. It starts:

"In the summer one day a Grasshopper was hopping about in a field. He was chirping and singing to himself. Suddenly a big black Ant scurried by, logging along an ear of corn he was taking to his colony.

'Will you not come and play with me,' said the Grasshopper, 'instead of working so hard all the time?'

'I have to prepare for the winter,' said the Ant, 'And why aren't you preparing?'

'Winter is far away,' said the Grasshopper. 'We have plenty of time. You must enjoy the summer while it lasts.' But the Ant shook his head and continued, determined, on his way.

"*As the winter months passed and the weather grew colder he kept meeting the grasshopper, who was starving and miserable. The ant was well fed and content because of the work he and the other ants had been doing over summer. Then the Grasshopper realized: It is best to prepare in advance.*

"Oh I know that story!" exclaimed Chris. "But I know a different version from Hungary. I tell it to the class. In the Hungarian version the grasshopper gets a better deal. It goes like this:

"*In the summer one day the grasshopper was playing the violin with his legs. The ant came along and stopped to listen for a moment. 'What fine music you make.'*

Of ants

'Come and listen and I will teach you how to play.' But the ant was too busy to stop and explained that he was busy storing food and had no time to spare. Then in the winter time, the ant came across the grasshopper who was bedraggled and very, very thin. *'Please help me! I am so hungry. I haven't eaten since the summertime.'* The ant felt so sorry for his friend that he welcomed him into his home with the other ants. *'You made such beautiful music for me that I want to look after you now.'*

"The grasshopper thanked him again and again. *'I will teach you all how to play the violin'* he said."

The ant orchestra

Jerome smiled: "Such a different meaning, and yet the stories are very similar. I can see how both stories carry a moral value and make a point. It is quite important to be sure of the point you want to make when using a story. Do you consider the implications of this when you tell stories to your class?"

"That is important," Chris agreed. "I like the version I tell to my class because it reminds them to share with each other, and that everyone has something of value that they can add. Although, in fact, the other version might be suitable for older children. You could use it to persuade them to prepare for exams!"

They both laughed.

Hidden messages

"You know what I was thinking? I might like to tell both ant stories to my class when I go home. Then the class could tell me what the two messages were and which they agreed with."

Jerome looked pleased. "I was also thinking that this might provide an opportunity for you to teach the class about the importance on reflecting on the values inherent in stories, and whether they wish to adopt them."

Chris said "You mean like making hidden messages clear to children? That happens in television too. I sometimes talk about TV adverts with the children and we discuss what the advertisers want them to believe."

With a slightly concerned glance at the children Jerome said "Yes, it is possible to distort facts using stories in the media, so it is important to give children the tools to distinguish facts from fiction. This is one of the objections to using stories in school, that children should learn the facts, and not be confused."

Alex exclaimed, pointing to the small PSP-screen. "Isn't that cute? This little ant is in his cradle with his mum looking after him."

Hidden messages

Jo looked scornful. "Ants don't have mums like that, idiot! There is a queen ant who has all the babies and the worker ants feed her and look after the little ants. But you wouldn't get an established queen looking after her own baby." With an air of great authority, he added "I read it on *Wikipedia*."

Jerome said. "You are very well informed I must say. Where did you say you read this?"

"*Wikipedia*. You know, the encyclopaedia on the internet?" elaborated Jo as Jerome still looked blank. "Anyone can put an entry in the encyclopaedia, or people can change it if they want to. You get lots of experts writing pages."

"Yes, if you can tell they're really experts," pointed out Chris. "I always tell my children to be careful when they are finding sources on the Internet. They could be written by anyone."

Jerome fingered his small neat beard. "It is not always easy to get meaning out of facts. Reading an encyclopaedia will not provide you with the full picture of what you need to know. Often you have to see things in a context or a greater perspective. This is what a story can do."

"But the story is wrong, so idiots like Alex think that it is real when it is not."

"I do not! I know it is a story, and they are still cute!"

Alex launched herself at Joe and started kicking him. Jo retaliated by pulling her hair as hard as he possibly could. He had had a lot of practice.

Modes of thought

After Chris had finally separated the children she sat down again and the conservation resumed when it was possible to hear above their argument.

"It is interesting," Jerome said, "that theorists say that actually there are two different modes of thought. One of the most famous is Bruner. He proposes that narrative and logico-scientific thinking are distinct modes [17]."

Chris looked slightly daunted. "What do you mean?" she asked politely.

Jerome looked pleased to be asked about his favourite subject. People who knew him well tended not to ask.

He leaned forward and adjusted his bow-tie before he ventured into his explanation.

"You see," he started, "the important thing is to understand that human thought unfolds in these different modes and is not that one mode is better than the other, only that the right mode should be applied for the right task. We have had a rather long period where the only acceptable mode is the logico-scientific. That means that formal education has been focused mainly on rational thinking, hypothesis testing, producing verifiable evidence and prizing encyclopaedic knowledge. What is valued here is theory, analysis, proof and categorisation and sound argument. It is a mode where there can be many competing theories which fit observations and have predictive power. It is a mode of establishing truth."

---

[17] Bruner, J. S. (1986). <u>Actual minds, possible worlds</u>. Cambridge, Mass., Harvard University Press.

Chris commented "Well, stories can have truth in them too, can't they?"

"Yes, but the truth you find in stories is different from scientific truth. In the story there is always a concrete situation where truth becomes manifest through its lifelikeness. Story truth is about the believability of the story while scientific truth is about discovering a universal truth, where the explanation is abstracted from a temporal and spatial context and of course not dependent on a person's particular situation. This lack of relation to particular circumstances shows no empathy and can make scientific theories feel cold-hearted."

"Maybe that is why Jo likes reading *Wikipedia*, while Alex likes the movie with the story about those particular characters. Does your theory say anything about how boys and girls respond to stories?" asked Chris.

"Well, in principle this applies to all human thought, rather than to just boys or girls. But what are your experiences?"

Chris thought for a moment then replied "Actually I think there is quite a difference between boys and girls here. As you could see, Alex was really getting interested in ants from this movie she was watching, while Jo obviously was quite proud of all he knew from his reading an encyclopaedia. I was at a talk not long ago, where a researcher like you was visiting my school, telling us about her project [18] on boys' and girls' reading interests. She said that her work with the kids had shown that boys like

---

[18] If you read Danish, see: Børn læser bøger : læsevaner, læsefærdighed, højtlæsning / Anette Steffensen og Torben Weinreich. - Kbh. : Roskilde Universitetsforlag, 2000. - 101 s. : ill. - (Skriftserie fra Center for Børnelitteratur ; 3)
Otherwise, try: Millard, E. (1997). Differently literate : boys, girls, and the schooling of literacy. London, Falmer Press.

reading non-fiction while girls enjoy fiction more. She suggested that we should get the boys to write non-fiction because it feels more motivating, while the girls prefer to write stories. It is not always true though, because I have a male colleague who thinks his boys' stories are more interesting than the ones his girls write. Maybe all that means is that boys like reading boys' stories!"

They both smiled, then Jerome continued on his favourite topic: "In stories you tend to make connections with things with which you are already familiar and have experienced. This is one of the reasons that stories can make good teaching tools. You can share your experiences in a way others can identify with."

Stories and culture

"I don't get this," said Alex suddenly to Jerome whom she seemed to have adopted as a dapper uncle figure. She was half way through her *Stories from Around the World* book and she had been showing him pictures she liked from time to time. This time, however, it was the story she didn't understand.

"It's about a girl who married a lion[19]," she explained. "She marries this man, and they have two sons but then her brother gets suspicious that her husband is really a lion. No-one believes him so he sets a trap for the husband by leaving a goat outside his house. In the morning all of the goat has been eaten apart from the

---

[19] McCall Smith, A. and N. Holwill (2005). Folk tales from Africa : the girl who married a lion. Edinburgh, Canongate.

bones. The brother says this means that it must have been eaten by the husband because only lions do that. All the family chase the husband (or lion, I suppose) and they see that he leaves behind paw prints instead of footsteps. The lady doesn't seem to mind that her husband was a lion, but then she gets worried that her sons might be lions too."

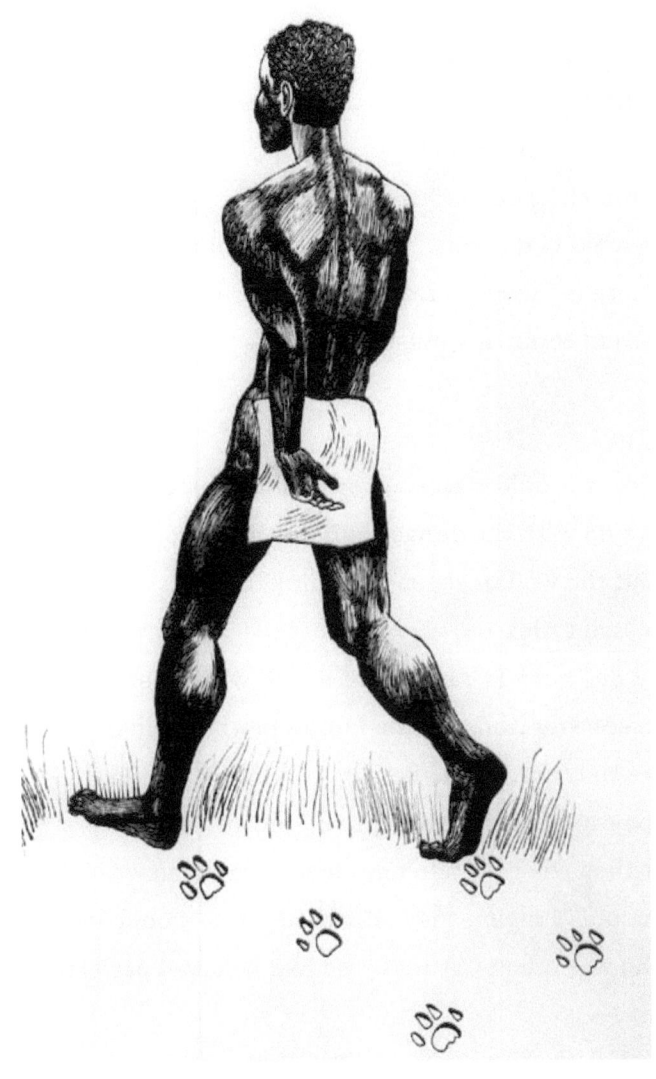

The lion man

"Naturally," said Jerome.

"Well, the brother puts the two little boys in a cage near where the real lions wander about. He tells them that he would like them to test whether the cage is lion proof. The boys are crying and scared, but he goes and hides in the bushes to see what will happen. The real lions do come, and they prowl round the cage and start roaring and jumping at the cage and trying to attack the boys! Finally the brother throws his spear at the lions and rescues the boys. He tells their mother they're not lions so she's quite pleased, and that's the end."

"Hmmmm," said Jerome.

"But what is it about?" she asked, "What does it *mean*?"

"Sometimes stories mean different things to different people, or in different countries. What country is the story from?" asked Jerome.

"Africa."

"Maybe it would mean something different to an African child who grows up with the danger of lions. Have you ever heard the story about the wolf in sheep's clothing?"

"No," said Alex.

"Oh I do," said Jo. "It's about a wolf who dresses up by putting a lamb fleece over him and the lamb's mother thinks the wolf is her lamb. And then it eats her."

"Appearances can be deceptive," put in Chris.

"But then the lion didn't eat his children, so was it fair to chuck him out? I mean, they only thought he would do bad stuff because he was a lion but really he had behaved perfectly nicely until then."

"Or maybe it means that danger can lurk in the heart of a family," pondered Jerome.

A wolf in sheep's clothing

Alex thought for a while.

"Well, I don't think the *uncle* was very nice," she said. "He seems like the dangerous one to me. Locking people up in cages like that."

"Still, you'll wonder about that story for a while now, won't you?" Jerome said, "Sometimes it's the stories which puzzle us which we feel a need to return to."

"I feel a need for another toffee," said Alex, meaningfully eying Jerome's bag of sweets.

Jerome handed her the bag while he continued talking to Chris. "I have always wondered about the different ways of understanding a story since I read an anthropology paper about a theatre company which travelled to Africa to perform Hamlet for an African tribe."

"Well, that's interesting," said Chris before she snatched the bag back from Alex, who was starting on her fourth toffee.

"The company was very surprised by the local African audience's reaction to the play. They actually could not understand that it was a problem for Hamlet that his mother had remarried the killer of his father, since that was the ancient custom in their tribe. So they thought that Hamlet was seriously mad about making such a fuss over the matter."

"Good Lord!" Chris exclaimed, thinking that she hadn't suspected that anthropology papers would have such juicy stories.

Multiple points of view

"I like my classes to think about how the different characters feel in a story though," Chris said. "A story can look quite different if you take the point of view of some other character, especially if there are conflicts between the characters. What if the Wolf in *Little Red Riding Hood* was the last wolf because all the rest of his pack had died of starvation? And he was too weak and hungry to chase deer and that's why he ate the grandmother? Does the story look different then?"

"That's just a different story," Jo said, scornfully. "You'd have to call it *The Starving Wolf,* not *Little Red Riding Hood.* Anyway, eating people is always bad if you're people."

Multiple points of view

"But different points of view are not just about characters," Jerome pointed out. "We've already agreed that stories often also have a cultural role."

"Oops," Chris thought, "another speech coming up."

"Stories can be used to persuade the listener that a single point of view is correct, or stories can be used to encourage the belief that multiple points of view are acceptable, and to be encouraged." Jerome continued "It depends on the beliefs educators have about the ways in which children should be taught."

"Of course," Chris agreed quickly. "We want our children to be tolerant and celebrate diversity. Asking them to think about the points of view of different characters helps them to be positive about other perspectives and cultures. But I know it wasn't always like that."

"That's because it can be seen as undermining shared values," Jerome responded. "For example, have you ever asked your children to think about how Noah's Flood affected all the people who didn't have an ark?"

"The dumbasses drowned of course," Jo told him. "They didn't take any notice of Noah when Noah was right."

"So thousands of children drowned because their parents had the wrong religious position?" Jerome asked ironically.

"But that makes it sound like God was a baddie," Alex said, worried.

"You see, that could be a bit controversial," Chris said, also sounding worried. "I could imagine some parents getting cross and I wouldn't want to send my kids home in tears."

"Educators are part of society so they too are influenced as to what is right, or, at least, preferable," Jerome said. "I also want children to grow up fairly tolerant of religious minorities, dyslexics, football players and so on. That makes me reluctant to use stories, for example, that portray the main protagonist as having racist tendencies or evident religious bigotry."

"It's true I don't use any stories like that either. But doesn't it depend what happens?" Chris asked. "There are lots of stories where the main character learns the error of his or her ways. Alex has some good examples in her *Stories Around the World*—can I just borrow it for a minute please Alex?"

Alex handed over the colourful and very thick volume.

"This one is really interesting," Chris said. "It's a Japanese story called *The man who did not wish to die*[20]. It's about a man who is lazy, and living on inherited money. He prays at a shrine to live forever and is transported to the island of Perpetual Life by a giant crane that springs into being from one made of paper. But he discovers that all the inhabitants want most of all to die and do everything they can to shorten their lives, though even if they take poisons it has no effect. After he has lived there for three hundred years it becomes totally monotonous and he prays just as hard to return to his old home. On the way back the crane turns back into paper and he falls into the sea and thinks he is about to drown, but before he can, he wakes up to find the whole thing was a dream. A messenger appears in a bright light and tells him to go home and live a good and industrious life and to forget his old bad ways, and in the end that is what he does."

---

[20] Ozaki, Y. T. The Japanese fairy book. Compiled by Yei Theodora Ozaki, Rutland.

Multiple points of view

"I hate that type of story," Jo grumbled. "It's like preaching at you. Of course nobody wants to die and that story isn't going to change anyone's mind."

"Stories with anti-heroes are not often intended to present multiple points of view," Jerome commented. "This is not only true of fiction of course. I cannot imagine teaching the history of pre-war Germany in which we ask children to take Hitler's point of view because in order to do so we would be asking them to look for arguments in favour of genocide. Nevertheless to understand the history of Germany requires more than studying history from the point of view of Germans. One would also have to consider the points of view of the Polish, French, British and so on—let alone the perspective of some of the minorities in Germany."

"Can I have my book back, Miss?" asked Alex, looking bored. Chris handed it back to her, thoughtfully. Alex retired into a corner with it in relief.

"One of the good things about stories though is that you can look at different points of view without getting involved in history or religion and upsetting people," Chris said.

"Yeah, but that's just kid's stuff," Jo told her. "Ok for Alex maybe, but paper cranes and talking rabbits are lame."

"I think that stories themselves may emphasise the need for multiple perspectives or effectively contradict it," Jerome mused. "For example, some 19th century educationalists had quite a narrow concept of what it meant to be a good person, and would not have wanted to use any story that challenged this view. So, a hero had to be good, and a villain, bad. If the leading character was one you should not approve of, then the story told you that quite directly. That was Jo's 'preaching'."

"Bit like you're doing now," Jo muttered. Chris gave him a sharp look and he went pink. "I think I'll get back to my PSP," he said, and went to sit next to Alex.

"People in society can exert strong pressures that permit, or forbid, certain points of view being expressed." Jerome continued, taking no notice of the interruption. "Those involved in education often seek to develop attitudes and opinions in children that are widely seen as positive. Many education systems currently seek to emphasise the acceptance of people with different physical and mental capabilities and from different cultures and religions. Stories can be used very effectively to do this. Other cultures may not be so keen to accept the value of multiple points of view as part of the education of its citizens. Those of us who want children to learn multiple points of view through stories have to face up to the fact that some points of view challenge our assumptions, and that some way needs to be found to accommodate the often necessary debate."

"I'm sure you're right," Chris said brightly.

A game of Barnga

A while later, Jo, who had been visiting another carriage, flung himself back into their compartment.

"I thought you said that was going to be a game," he said to Chris accusingly.

"But I left you playing cards," Chris said. "Did something go wrong?"

"You mean apart from everyone nearly coming to blows?" Jo asked.

"Goodness me, do I need to go back and help?" Chris asked anxiously. She'd left Jo in a compartment further down the train where a Year 7 class were about to play a card game. She'd hoped that some time out with kids closer to his own age would give Jo a breather from his little sister, and from Jerome's grave discussions.

"Oh, it's all cool, we sorted it out in the end," Jo said. "But it wasn't so much a card game as a way of messing with our heads. Though maybe not in a bad way in the end."

"Messing with your heads?" Jerome asked, sounding confused.

"Making you think, that type of stuff," Jo told him.

"But what happened?" Chris asked him. "When I left they were splitting you up into groups of four and I thought you were going to play Whist or something like that."

"Well, I wouldn't have hit anyone," Alex interjected. "Can I go and play cards now?" She had been most put out when Chris had told her Jo was playing cards with a whole new group of kids.

"You just wouldn't have got it," Jo told her in a superior tone. "To make someone think they have to have a brain in the first place."

"I would so."

"If it made you think, *what* did it make you think?" Jerome asked quickly.

"After they put us into groups of four, we got a piece of paper about the game." Jo responded. "It was sort-of Whist," he said, turning to Chris. "I had one of the other three as my partner, and you had to cut the pack for who was to deal. Spades were trumps, and then you'd each play a card and the highest would win the trick unless there was a trump. But like you couldn't trump people if you had a card of the suite the person before you had played. The only different bit was that we were all told we couldn't talk. Though I thought that was just to keep the noise down a bit. Then when you'd finished you counted up the tricks to see which partners had won, and then the next person round on the right would deal."

"Were you playing for matchsticks or something?" Chris asked, unable to work out why this could have led to anyone coming to blows.

"No, just to see who won more games," Jo said. "Well, after a while they told us all to stop and then said that the winning partners from each group should move to the next group round. Me and my partner had wiped the floor in our group, so we got to move. So then we started playing with this new pair of people."

"And you couldn't talk to them either?" Chris asked, beginning to guess what might have happened.

"Yeah, that turned out to be important. Well. Me and my partner were storming away again, and I put down an ace, which is the highest you can get, and then the guy next to me put down the king on top and then tried to grab the trick. 'Cheeky monkey,' I thought, and I tried to grab it back, and he looked really cross, and we had a sort of a tug of war. So just as well we couldn't say anything at that point or they'd have been telling us off for bad language, but I gave him a real glare and in the end he backed down. But then his partner got involved, and she grabbed the trick off our pile, and then my partner tried to grab it off her and it all got a bit messy. And then I noticed that the next group were having some kind of a barney too, and it was like a little light went on in my brain."

"What do you mean?" asked Jerome, sounding even more confused.

"Say that each group got a different set of rules on their bit of paper," Jo said triumphantly. "You'd never know until your pair moved into another group. And then you'd never know until you hit something where they had a different rule from you."

"And is that what happened then? Why would they do that?" asked Chris, wondering who would set up a situation so likely to lead to trouble.

"So at that point the teacher in charge told us to stop playing," Jo said. "Just as well really. It looked as if things were getting a bit out of hand in some of the groups. Then she asked us what we thought it would be like when we got to the festival given it's so far from home. Would people possibly have different ways of doing things from the way we were used to and how would we feel about that?"

"Oh, I see!" said Chris, a little light going on in her brain too.

"Of course!" said Jerome. "Experiential learning!"

"What learning?" asked Jo, puzzled.

"Sometimes it's quite easy to learn something by reading about it," Jerome told him. "For example, you can learn how to do an experiment in chemistry by following some written-down instructions. But other things you have to experience—for example you cannot learn to ride a bike by reading instructions, you really have to try it."

"Cool," Jo said. "So they made us experience a different culture by giving us different rules for the same thing and mixing us up."

"Precisely," Jerome told him. "In fact you really will experience a different culture when we get to the festival. That is one of the educational outcomes of sending you all there, I imagine. But it's usually quite difficult to give people that experience in the classroom. Not only that, as you saw in your groups, when people operate by different rules without realising it, they can get quite angry with each other. Each thinks their rule is 'the' rule and that the other person is deliberately breaking it."

"Yeah, I thought the guy next to me was cheating," Jo replied. "I suppose it's better to have the bust-up in a game than in real-life though."

"I suppose so," Chris said dubiously, thinking how hard it might be to deal with a whole classroom full of groups falling out.

"It's one of the advantages of role-play," Jerome added. "Drama can give people quite intense emotional experiences in a much safer environment than the real world. By talking about the experience afterwards, people incorporate what they've learned into their own personal story."

"We had a really good discussion about it," Jo agreed. "We've done other cultures in class, but I didn't realise just how stressful it can be if people are working by different rules from yours. Almost as stressful as kid sisters."

Storytelling in the curriculum

Alex had settled down again with her storybook, and Chris felt it would be OK to leave her there with Jerome and Jo while she went to get some lunch. Ada was still asleep in the corner and seemed unlikely to wake anytime soon. She went down the corridor and opened the door into the restaurant car. The car was full with schoolchildren buying snacks and fizzy drinks.

She noticed a free seat next to a friendly looking man with red hair and freckles, so she asked if she could sit down.

"Please," he grinned, "I could do with some adult company."

"Oh," Chris said, "are you travelling with these children?"

He grimaced, "Unfortunately." He extended a hand. "I'm Peter, and I'm a teacher with Riverbank School. I teach Year 7."

Chris shook his hand. "I'm a teacher as well. But I'm teaching Year 4 this year. I'm going to a Future of Learning Conference. I was asked to look after one of my class, Alex, and her brother Jo, because they are coming along too, since Alex has been chosen to perform a poem she wrote as part of a story-telling project we've been doing. It's such an exciting trip for them. They've been as high as kites!"

"That's a coincidence. My class is here to go the Future of Learning too. We won a competition on the best video-documentary on bio-diversity. My children are 11 so they are too old for stories."

Chris was not going to let this past. "Too old for stories? You're never too old for stories! I used to work with children in Year 7 and they were very appreciative of stories. We did some great story projects together."

"What kind of things did you do?"

"I used it in a term-long project. We were learning about stories, and about animals I suppose. Do you know the story of Anansi and the Sky Blue Box of Stories?"

Peter looked taken aback "Can't say I do," he said, as the waitress brought his cup of coffee.

"I do," said the waitress unexpectedly. "I used to read it to my children." She was a comfortable looking middle aged woman, wearing a green overall with a name badge: Claire. Chris noticed her laughter lines. "Storyteller's eyes," she thought.

"That's fantastic," she said, "Do you read to them a lot?"

"Oh yes," she said. "My girl is ten now and she just loves them."

She explained to Peter "It's the story of Anansi the spider man."

Peter looked even more confused. "Spider man?" he said. "As in the comic guy?"

"No," said Claire, "He's a character from African stories. He is a trickster like Brer Rabbit. You must know Brer Rabbit."

"Errrr."

"Anyway," said Claire, taking pity on him. "Anansi discovers that the Sky God is keeping all the stories of the world in a big box, and he has to do all these tasks before the Sky God will give him the stories. Of course his wife helps him with all his tasks."

Chris nodded with approval.

"When he has done them, he gets the box of stories, but he drops it on the way down from Heaven and all the stories fly out all over the world and this is why you have stories. My kids want that one again and again. Even my boy, who's a bit younger."

Storytelling in the curriculum

Anansi and the sky blue box of stories

"Exactly. Well, there is also a version where you have to find all stories and bring them to back to the box again. So my class went out to collect stories. I asked them to collect animal stories: you know like how the leopard got his spots."

Claire smiled and started clearing the coffee-cups. "I'm glad to hear *some* teachers know that stories are important." She said with a pointed glance at Peter as she moved away.

Peter wasn't going to take this lying down. "Well, are they?" he challenged Chris. "I mean the curriculum is so crowded. There are so many things we have to teach. I remember back to training college. One of the lecturers always told us: we had to prioritize. It seems to me that the facts are more important than stories, but what do you think?"

"Stories are tremendously important. Facts are important too, of course, and sometimes children will tell you facts which they have learned through stories. And after all, there is more to learning than knowing facts."

"But isn't there a risk of confusing the children if you mix facts and fiction? Like with the leopard and the spots. That story doesn't tell you anything about evolution, does it?"

Chris agreed "No, it doesn't tell you about evolution, but it does tell you about relationships and in some stories it can also tell you about the habitat, like in Kipling's story, and when you understand the conditions in the jungle, you'll better understand the camouflage that the Leopard developed. Once you understand the characters and the setting it can prepare the ground for more scientific thinking."

She thought to herself: "If Jerome were here, I'm sure he would say something about those modes of thought, but it's more than I want to bring up over a cup of coffee."

Peter was willing to listen, especially to someone as attractive as Chris. He wasn't necessarily convinced though.

"What would you say the benefits would be then? What do the kids get out it?"

"In a classroom there is always somebody who has a difficult time getting on with it. Now the politicians tell us to have an inclusive school, but when it comes down to it, it can be very difficult to make thirty kids interested and progress at the same rate."

Peter nodded. "That's true," he said, "but what do stories have to do with that? You still need to read and write to get started, don't you?"

Storytelling in the curriculum

"Telling a story can be a way into written literacy. If you use a story that catches the children's interest it's amazing how much better they concentrate and work. It's almost like magic. Sometimes you see even the most disruptive children just completely absorbed in the story world. And you know, those kinds of 12 year olds who think they are terribly grown-up hang on every word too. They are like proper children again."

"Oh, I've got a few kids like that in my class."

"I've even had a few dyslexic kids who were really having a difficult time with ordinary class, since they felt they never really could do anything well enough. I think they just felt stupid. I had one boy who said to me, 'Miss Headington, I love stories, because there is no wrong.' I think he meant that in other subjects he always got the wrong answer. But when he was free to make up his own stories, and tell them to the class, it was amazing to see that he actually was capable of making and sustaining very complex storylines. The other children loved what he had to say. That made such a difference that he finally felt adequate and accepted. I heard from his other teachers that he had made such progress in their subjects as well."

Peter warmed to her enthusiasm "What curriculum areas would it be relevant to work with? What would I tell my head-teacher?"

Chris had rehearsed this answer for her own head teacher. "Talking and listening, writing, personal and social development," she said promptly.

He sighed. "I always find it hard to do talking and listening with them. I mean, they are fine with talking! But listening? That's a different story."

"I had a storyteller friend who always used to tell me 'the best storytellers are the best listeners.' I turned it into a catch phrase for the class. Of course, your students may be used to passively listening to the television or radio, but it is really the presence of the storyteller that makes the difference. Last year I visited the Storytelling Centre in Scotland which has a phrase imprinted on the glass of one of the windows. It says 'Stories are told eye to eye, mind to mind and heart to heart.' I think that's true. The kids concentrate and absorb the stories so well when there is that personal connection between the storyteller and the audience."

"I could never tell stories," said Peter "I was always rubbish at drama in school."

"Come on, I'm sure you would be wonderful! Look at me, even though I'm no actor if I choose a story that really means something to me it also resonates with the class and I have no trouble keeping their attention. I'm sure you would enjoy it if you gave it a go. It's the story which is the centre of attention. Not you. The story tells itself."

"Mmm," he said. "Maybe it's like when I am working with the children on the film project. It seems natural to me, and the children are all concentrating on putting together the film. They are not waiting for me to say something clever. I am just helping them out because I am more experienced."

"You see?" Chris smiled. "I knew you would be creative with the children. They must have been really inspired by your film project."

Peter was beginning to get swept along with this woman's conviction. "Maybe I could try it," he murmured. "Why not?"

Storytelling in the curriculum

"My experience of using stories in the classroom has been pretty similar to that. My children have been able to work on their own—independent learning—because they were into their own stories and they related to a common theme which kept the process together. Also, they were good at helping each other. They were peer tutoring, so I had more time to help the ones that were really in need of my attention. And it was nice just to spend time with the children to discover their ideas."

"If I wanted to do a story-project with my class, how would I get started?" he asked.

Chris said "It's like any other project. I start of thinking what the learning goals are and how much time I have. And then when I know what area of the curriculum I want to cover, I start planning it with a story in mind. You can work with stories in different ways, but I can tell you about a project I recently did to give you an idea of how easily it can be done."

"That would be great!" said Peter.

"With this particular project I wanted them to learn about environmental studies and cover the marine life part of the curriculum. I personally believe in subjects supporting each other so I was happy when I could integrate art and literacy with the science aspect because it tends to make it more interesting to the children. It motivates them. I was so lucky that it coincided with a visiting art teacher. That added to the project but I could have done it anyway. I remembered hearing a story about a mermaid which kind of stuck in my mind. I thought it would be nice to tell the children that to get started, and then use it as a theme for the rest of the project."

"Where did you find the story?"

"I vaguely remembered it, but not all the details so I went to the library and looked through children's anthologies. That can be a great help."

"You could have looked online, maybe."

Chris made a face. "Computers and me don't mix. Some of my kids find stories online though."

Peter said "Would any story do? Or does it have to be a fairy tale or something?"

"Any story will do. The important thing is that the story-world will be consistent with the teaching you want to do."

"How do I know that, though?"

"Maybe you will have to try out a story project to appreciate the possibilities and once you have done that then you will have a much better feeling for it."

"What kind of lessons would you plan?"

Chris pulled a red folder out of her bag. "Look. Here are my notes from this sea project. I brought them in case I needed them for the conference"

Peter looked over her shoulder. "I see. You've got your introduction session where you told the story. Then a discussion about what the story meant. Yup, and then brain storming for story ideas—I do brain storming with my class too. So you got the kids to make up their own stories? Did they write them down?"

"Not until later on. They did a lot of preparation first."

"Oh right. I see you went to the sea life centre. I think I've been there with my class too, but it was all science stuff."

"They learned science too," said Chris, thinking of Alex's shark knowledge which so impressed her brother.

Storytelling in the curriculum

"And library research too, on this lesson where they found other sea stories. This is really good. I can begin to see how this might work. It's not just about stories at all, is it?"

"The stories are the launching point for all kinds of other things. It hooks them in, and then they can develop their own interests. Visual art, or maybe drama, or science even. I think what's really important is that they get to express themselves."

They looked through the folder together for a while.

"Were you interested in learning theories when you were at college?" she asked.

"I was really into constructivist learning. It makes sense to me that people learn best when they direct their own learning and try to make sense of new concepts through their own experience. Then of course, the teacher is meant to set up learning opportunities and facilitate learning as it occurs. I just sometimes find it difficult to actually do it. It seems to take so much preparation and maybe we need equipment that the school doesn't have and it seems to get daunting quite quickly."

"The beauty of this type of learning with stories is that you can easily involve everybody and they are all being little constructers" she chuckled. "You don't really need much that isn't in the classroom already."

"I can see how you would extend it though, if you had some computers or a video camera. You could do an animation story. They would love that!"

"What do you mean by animation?"

Peter was glad to be able to share some of his experience. Her opinion of him was beginning to matter quite a lot. "You probably know the big animated films by Disney or Pixar, but many people don't realize that you can actually make similar animations dead easily. You just need a computer and a camera, and then you can animate simple figures which the children have made. In that way I had them make an animation of the Food Chain which is part of the video we will be showing at the Conference. You should come along and see that."

"I would love to," she said. "But I don't know how to use a video camera, and my computer keeps crashing and then I get stressed."

"I would be happy to help you there," he said, spotting a chance. "I'll give you my email address and you can let me know if you get stuck"

"I don't use email," she said.

"Here's my number then," he said. "I'd like to find out more about the sea project too. Can I come to the exhibition?"

"Ok," she gave in to his persistence. "See you later then." she said as she finished her drink.

He watched her walk down the corridor again. This journey was full of surprises.

Sugar coated sea monsters

All was calm when Chris got back to the carriage. Jo was playing a game on his console and Jerome appeared to be drawing a picture of a mermaid for Alex to colour in. Both Ada and Alex (miracle of miracles) were asleep.

"That's nice picture, Jerome," said Chris wickedly. "Are you going to put it on your fridge when you get home?"

Jerome looked a little abashed, but continued to draw. In fact he was pondering on the question of authenticity. He had been reading an increasing number of papers in which researchers would state that they were exploring learning in 'authentic contexts' or that the activities that they were asking children to complete were 'authentic', but he wondered what this really meant. His reflections had also been fuelled by the earlier conversation about experiential learning and he was now pondering about what would make a story authentic? Some stories are authentic for their readers, because those readers have a close relationship to the setting of the story, or because they can relate to the characters in the story. Other stories might be considered authentic because the reader can make a personal connection with the purpose, or perhaps the moral of the story. Stories might also be considered to be authentic examples of the culture of the authors. These aspects of authenticity would have great value in certain sorts of learning. He considered authentic learning in other parts of the curriculum, which prompted him to ask Chris:

"How do you make learning maths authentic for your class?"

Chris looked up from her magazine. "What?" she said, "Oh right. I do try to make sure that I introduce mathematics concepts in a way that helps children relate what they are learning to what they do in their lives."

"Yes, but how do you know what is *authentic* for a particular child?" Jerome queried.

"Some things are quite safe bets really. For example, shopping is something that all of them experience to some extent, either by going into the shops or nowadays by using the internet. So they need to know how to choose the best deal when they see they can get 50% discount in one shop and 'buy one get one free' in another."

"I can see that, but how do you make sure that the children understand the principles so that they can apply what they have learnt about shopping and discounts in this activity to different shops or to different situations such as being able to increase the ingredients in a recipe by 50%?" pressed Jerome.

"That's a good question and we do use lots of different examples to help here. But for some children who struggle with maths, being able to shop is an important skill and I sometimes wonder if it is enough that they can do that even if they don't understand all the maths."

Jerome went back to his drawing for a moment, while he thought. He was very much of the belief that the Holy Grail of education is to help people to transfer what they learn from one context to another. Some of his academic colleagues would have agreed with Chris that the objective of learning was being able to complete an activity when the need arises in normal life. Others favoured approaches to learning that put more emphasis on being able to abstract the maths from the situation so that it could be generalized and applied in another different situation.

"I wonder about that," he said.

Chris put her magazine aside again with a sigh. Clearly she was not going to get peace to read it after all. Jerome took this as an invitation to continue "There was some classic research that explored the cultural nature of maths understanding. The researchers looked at situations where, because of economic necessity, commercial transactions formed the basis for even young children's maths activities and understandings. Basically they found that these children developed mathematical systems that worked well for their particular needs, such as selling candy on the streets of Brazil. However, whilst the maths knowledge and skills that these learners gained through these everyday activities could be used flexibly in their particular practice, it was of limited use in other contexts."[21]

Chris felt a little intimidated by being told about this research.

"It's not fair," she thought miserably, "I do make sure the kids understand their basic maths concepts. *And* I only wanted to read my magazine." If only she could put this across to Jerome.

"But I... we... I don't know about Brazil but..."

She looked around the carriage for inspiration. Jo was playing on his games console again, and this reminded her how technology could sometimes help.

"We also use computers to help with maths and sometimes the computer presents children with a real activity, such as shopping or whatever. Other times it is a game with rewards and levels."

"I can see that computers could be used in this way," agreed Jerome. "I can imagine that this could be very engaging for children especially if there is a story that underpins this experience. But do the children learn maths this way or do they just learn to play the game?"

Chris was just about to answer when Jo said triumphantly "Ah, so you're back, I know how to sort you!"

---

[21] Nunes, T., A. D. Schliemann, et al. (1993). <u>Street mathematics and school mathematics</u>. Cambridge, Cambridge University Press.

Both she and Jerome turned to look at Jo and the game he was playing on his console. Lots of small sea monsters were invading the screen of the device and Jo seemed to be fending them off using a variety of different weapons. Sometimes he caught the monsters in a net and they disappeared into a chest with many compartments; sometimes Jo defended himself against the monster and it disappeared; and then on other occasions Jo defended himself and the monster grew bigger and attacked Jo again.

"Clearly Jo has a very good knowledge about this game," Jerome noted to himself, his interest sharpening. "He can remember when he encounters the same type of monster again and knows what each of the weapons is capable of doing."

Gradually after watching for a while, Jerome realised that each of the monsters had particular features such as number of legs and heads or tails and that what Jo was actually doing was categorising them into the chest, getting rid of the ones that did not fit into the categorisation scheme he was currently using.

Jerome wrote in his ever-present researcher's notebook: "The monsters that grow bigger must be the result of Jo making an error in this categorisation process. But can Jo use these categorisation skills outside of the game?"

"Jo," he called, "Can you tell me what is happening in the game?"

Jo was so engrossed that he did not hear Jerome. So Jerome asked again and tapped Jo on the shoulder this time too, just for good measure.

"Hang on, just let me finish this level," said Jo, irritated.

Sugar coated sea monsters

"Oh bum... what did you say?" he asked as he was swallowed by a sea monster.

"Can you explain the game to me?" asked Jerome.

"There are lots of sea monsters and you have to put them in these chests. To do that you need to use the right weapon to fight the monster," explained Jo.

"But how do you know which weapon to use?"

"Well you have to work it out by trying things," said Jo.

"How do you know what to try?"

"You have to come up with a plan. In that game I just played I thought that the monsters with long legs were all ones that must be cut into two pieces, so I use the knives with two blades on them. Then the monsters with big heads and tentacles must be cut into four pieces to be sorted so I used the bommy-knocker with four points. I thought that the big green slimy looking ones with those funny hair like things on their back need to be stabbed just once so I was using the dagger, but now I am not sure..."[22] Jo was still thinking about this.

Jerome realized that the game was about division and wondered if Jo had figured this out. Had the sea monster setting disguised the learning? Would Jo be able to apply his skills in a different context? He remembered a paper he had read a few months before. He explained to Chris "I was wondering about the value of Jo's game for maths education. It reminded me of a study I read which evaluated whether children were able to transfer learning from maths games to other maths activities. They did find

---

[22] This game bears an uncanny resemblance to a game called *Zombie Division*, created by Jake Habgood. See: Habgood, M. P. J., S. E. Ainsworth, et al. (2005). "Endogenous fantasy and learning in digital games." <u>Simulation Gaming</u> **36**(4): 483-498.

it difficult, although a class session with the teacher that talked about the game and about the maths in it was very effective in helping the children make the transfer, as I recall."

Chris was delighted by this last comment and remarked "That makes a lot of sense to me. I can see how a game like that would be useful, but of course they still need support from a teacher or a parent to make sense of it and apply it to their other learning."

She turned to Jo. "Do you think that the storyline with the sea monsters helps you with the maths?" she asked.

"Nah," said Jo. "Division is easy—I don't need help! The game is fun, but it doesn't really have a storyline, just a bunch of sea monsters. I don't see why you need to keep putting stories in everything anyhow. With maths, half the time they're not even proper stories. Look at all those maths problems with ladders and baths in them. 'A window cleaner has a 3 metre long ladder and has to clean a window two metres up. What angle does he need to lean it against the wall?' They just want you to do some math and it's to make you feel better about it. Like taking the nasty medicine with a sugar lump."

"That's a very good point with which I must agree," Jerome told him. Jo looked a bit surprised, and Chris revised her opinion of Jerome's good sense upwards. "That really is not a story in any sense of the term. More a case of window-dressing as you say."

"So why bother?" Jo asked. "Why not just get straight down to the problem?"

"But you just played that sea monsters game for a while," Chris pointed out. "Maybe the sugar lumps really did help you to take the nasty medicine." She thought that a program that could engage Jo for as long as that must be good.

"That of course was the point I was making," Jerome told her. "Even if the story is really just a background, if it is sufficiently engaging it can have a real effect on motivation."

"The sea monsters game doesn't have a real story," Jo countered. "It's like puzzles really. Or maths problems. But cool problems."

"From what I saw," Jerome commented, "The sea monsters were just graphical critters. If they had been given distinct personalities, and perhaps some feelings about the adventure, would it have made it seem more like a story?"

"I guess," said Jo slowly. "But problems are what math and science are about. Making the monsters more like story characters wouldn't have helped with the problems—you really had to just think about those without worrying about story-stuff. Stories are OK for History and English but I think they just get in the way in Maths."

"Have you ever come across the 'Mr Tompkins' stories?[23]" Jerome asked Jo.

Jo shook his head, but Chris remembered one of the lecturers at teacher training college talking about them.

"Aren't those stories about physics?" she asked. "Teaching quantum physics through shooting tigers who don't stay in one place?"

"That's right," Jerome told her. "Mr Tompkins had to hunt tigers in a world in which Planck's constant was much larger than in our universe. As a result the position of a tiger was noticeably uncertain the way the position of an electron is in our world. It did

---

[23] Gamow, G. (1993). Mr Tompkins in paperback, Cambridge University Press.

make it hard to shoot one successfully. I think stories do have a definite role in helping one understand physical principles because it is possible to dramatise what are otherwise rather abstract ideas."

"If it means shooting things maybe I'll give it a go," Jo said, smiling.

Chris returned to her magazine. Jerome went back to his notebook. He wrote: "While stories and technology can offer learners contextualised or authentic tasks which are motivating, this is *not* enough on its own to lead to learning. Simple sugar coating with stories or games may distract the learner from the heart of the problem they are trying to solve, and learners may subsequently find it hard to transfer their learning. So we must be careful in using stories or technology as simple motivators, and we must bear in mind the role that teachers have in supporting the transfer of knowledge from one situation to another."

Alex woke up. "Have you finished my drawing yet Jerome?"

"Not yet," said Jerome guiltily, putting down his fountain pen and picking up his crayon.

Princesses can be heroic too

Alex had been working through her world fairytales book for much of her journey.

"Why is it that so many of the stories have boys as heroes? Boys are stupid."

Princesses can be heroic too

Jo snatched the book and hit her over the head with it. "Isn't it obvious?" he said, flexing his muscles.

"No," snapped Chris who had had this conversation with many of the boys in her class before.

Alex continued "Think about Rapunzel. She doesn't do very much. She has really long hair, and she just leans out the window with it," she said derisively.

"You're just jealous because yours looks like a rat has been chewing it!" Jo returned.

Alex chose to ignore him for once. "And then there is Cinderella. Why doesn't she complain about all the work she has to do? I would."

"I know! You are always complaining when Mum tells you to tidy your room."

"And her sisters are really horrible..."

"Sisters *are* really horrible."

"...and her step mum is horrid too. That doesn't seem fair to me. My friend Anna has a step mum and she is really nice, not like Snow White's step mum. Stepmothers really don't go around poisoning people, do they?"

"No," said Chris firmly.

In the corner of the carriage Ada finally awoke. She untangled herself from her headphones, winked at Alex and went to get a cup of coffee.

Chris said "How about I tell you a story about a heroine?"

"Yes!" said Alex immediately.

"Oh, God here we go..." groaned Jo, who sensed feminism was on the cards.

Jerome was more polite "Oh please do."

Inside Stories: A Narrative Journey

Chris started:

"Once upon a time, there was a Princess who lived in a castle. Her name was Elizabeth. She had a boyfriend called Ronald. She loved Ronald because he was so handsome and so strong, and very brave indeed. She couldn't wait to marry him. On the day when this story starts, Elizabeth was sitting on her throne, watching Ronald comb his golden curls. All of a sudden, there was a blast of hot air, and the sound of flapping wings. The room darkened and in flew a dragon!

'Arrrgh!' shouted Ronald and dived behind Elizabeth's throne.

'Oi!' shouted Elizabeth, shaking her fist at the dragon. 'Stop that! You're making a mess.'

"And sure enough, the throne room was covered in dust and plaster. So was Elizabeth, but Ronald, hiding under the throne, had managed to keep himself clean. Not a curl was out of place.

"The dragon swooped down and tried to catch one of the servants. Elizabeth hit him over the head with her golden mace. 'Stop it, you big bully!"

"The dragon decided that this was all too much work and swooped over the throne where Ronald was cowering. With a snarl and a flame he snatched Ronald and flew out the window and away.

'Ronald!' wailed Princess Elizabeth.

"She sat down on the floor, surrounded in all the dust and mess, and started to cry. But not for long. In a moment, she sat up and wiped her face, leaving tear marks in the soot.

'Ronald, I'm going to rescue you!' she announced and marched for the door.

'Elizabeth! Stop! You can't possibly go!' cried her servant.

Princesses can be heroic too

'Of course I can. And I will.'

'But your dress...'

"Elizabeth looked down. She hadn't noticed before, but her dress was ripped and torn into so many shreds that you could see her pants."

Alex giggled. Jo blushed.

"'You can't go out like that.'

'Alright' said Elizabeth and looked round the room for something—anything—that she could wear. She saw a big brown paper bag which the baker had brought the buns in that morning. She made a neck hole and two arm holes and scrambled inside. 'Now I'm ready,' she said and set off.

"She walked for a long time until she got to the Dragon's house. She banged on the door and called 'Oh, Mr Dragon! Oh lovely Mr Dragon!'

"Inside the dragon stirred. He had never heard such a friendly greeting from such a pretty young lady.

'Yes Princess?'

'Oh Mr Dragon, I have heard that you can fly very fast. So fast that you can fly right round the world in a minute. Is that true Mr Dragon?'

'Why yes, Princess darling'

'Would you do it for me?' she batted her eyelids.

"The dragon was only too pleased to show off his beautiful iridescent wings, so he flapped mightily, took off and flew round the world in less time than it takes for me to tell you about it.

"He came back slightly out of breath, and said 'See Princess? See?'

'Oh yes, Mr Dragon! That was wonderful. Could you do it again for me?'

"The dragon was middle aged, and maybe had put on a little weight recently so he groaned at the thought of doing all that again. But the princess was so sweet and he wanted to impress her, so he did it. And again and again and again, until he was quite worn out. He collapsed in a giant heap of sweaty scales at Elizabeth's feet, snoring.

"Elizabeth tiptoed around him into his house. She saw Ronald tied up beside a cooking pot. Miraculously, he looked the same as ever. Not a golden curl was out of place.

'Elizabeth! What a mess you're in!'

'Oh, Ronald, Ronald! Are you alright?' she asked running to start untying him.

'But look at you! Where is your crown? Your hair is all tangled and your face is sooty and you're wearing …Well it looks like a paper bag!'

Princesses can be heroic too

The Paper Bag Princess

"Elizabeth looked at him. And she thought of all the effort she had been to so far. And she said 'Oh well Ronald, let's see how you get on without me.' And she left the ropes as they were, and skipped out of Mr Dragon's house, stepped over the sleeping dragon and ran happily down the hill into the sunset. The End."

Alex laughed. "I liked that story," she said.

Chris said "Alex, if you want to read that story at home, you should get the book. It's called the *Paper Bag Princess*, and it's by Robert Munsch[24]."

Jerome asked "Was that verbatim from the original text?"

---

[24] Munsch, R. N. and M. Martchenko (1980). The paper bag princess. London, Little Hippo, 1999.

"Do you mean, did I learn all the words by heart?" she replied. She was trying to train him to speak plainly. "No, of course not. I remember the bones of the story and put flesh on my own way."

"The bones of the story. What exactly do you mean?"

"The main parts of the plot, the development of the core action, as you would call it."

Jo looked sullen, "That's one stupid dragon," he said.

Alex countered "That's one vain prince."

Jerome added "There you go, that was the evaluation structural element for your story!"

Ada, who had come back with her cup of coffee halfway through the story, laughed too. "Great story," she said, "I think I know a Ronald."

Chris smiled at Ada "I really like stories that have strong females as characters. I think it is so important for the kids that they get a balanced view of the possibilities for women. Girls need strong role-models too."

"I agree," said Ada. "I once went to a seminar on women in folklore. Apparently there are different wonder-tales across the world where the heroine liberates men. Actually, they often liberate their brothers who for various reasons have been turned into polar bears, snakes, birds and that sort of thing. I dunno if I would have bothered rescuing my brother though. He would look good as a polar bear."

"What do you mean, she liberates them?" Chris asked.

"Well they were all bewitched and turned into animal shapes, and it was only the sister who could save them. This gives a different sort of view of the female role, doesn't it? Do you know the story of a girl who saves her seven brothers?"

Princesses can be heroic too

Nobody did, so Ada continued:

"*Once upon a time, there was a poor peasant who had seven sons but no daughters, and he so wished for one. Finally after many years his wife bore him a daughter, but she was sick and they feared they might lose her, so they were to have an emergency christening. He sent his sons to fetch water for the ceremony from a nearby spring—but each was so eager to get the water that they dropped the jug in the well, and then they dared not go home without the water and without the jug. The father was waiting for them to come back, and when they did not return, he thought they had forgotten about it and gone off to play and in his anger he called out a curse 'I wish that all the boys turn into black ravens.'*

"*As soon as he uttered that curse he heard the sound of wings in the air and above him he saw seven ravens fly away towards the mountains.*

"*When the sister had grown up she discovered that she had once had brothers. She was sitting in the kitchen and overheard an old woman talking about them, saying that it was good that she did not know that she indirectly had caused them to be banished. She made a vow to find them and set out on her quest. First she came to the Sun and when she asked for help, the Sun burned her badly and refused help but she did not give up and continued to find the Moon and ask her for help. The Moon was no more helpful and very cold to her, so she nearly froze to death, but she did not give up and continued her quest. When she reached the Stars they were friendly and gave her a chicken bone, which she should use to help her brothers.*

"*She then continued her quest until she came to the Mountain of Glass, and there was a door where she was to use her chicken* bone to open the lock. But she had lost it, and in order to enter she had to cut off one of her fingers and use that instead."

Alex interrupted "Ew! That sounds terrible. Couldn't she just have found another chicken?"

"Shh," Chris whispered "It was a gift from the Stars. Be quiet."

"What about just getting a key then?" said Jo practically.

"But it is a glass mountain..." said Alex.

"Yes, you can't enter a glass mountain with an ordinary key," said Chris as if stating the obvious.

Ada glared. "When you're ready," and then she continued:

"When the sister entered the mountain she was greeted by a dwarf, who told her that her brothers would be back later. She then went around the table he had set for them and took a little sip of each cup and in the last cup she dropped her mother's ring. When the brothers came home they said: 'Who had been drinking from my goblets?'"

"Just like Goldilocks," said Alex.

Jerome said "Isn't it interesting how you can recognize themes and patterns of stories? This reminds me of a study I once made of how oral storytellers make their stories. They actually improvise based on a number of story elements[25]. This is a very ancient tradition that you can find traces of in parts of Europe. For example the ballad singers use a formula, and a set of themes when they perform their long epic narratives."

---

[25] Lord, A. B., S. A. Mitchell, et al. (2000). The singer of tales. Cambridge, Mass. ; London, Harvard University Press.

Princesses can be heroic too

Chris commented "I once saw a Turkish storyteller who told a huge long story, but I heard that his longest story lasted for more than 12 hours."

Ada was beginning to get impatient. "This story will last for 12 hours if you don't let me finish it."

"I know how it ends" said Alex.

"Well why don't you finish it then?" said Ada, giving up.

The raven brothers

"The brothers find the ring in the cup. They know it belongs to their mother, and that it is their sister who has come to break the spell. They call out: 'Dear sister, are you here?', and then she comes out from her hiding place, and in that very moment the spell is broken." said Alex.

"How did you know that?" asked Ada in surprise.

"I just read the story in my world fairy tales book," Alex said smugly, enjoying being the centre of attention.

Jo scowled, and whispered to himself "That's not fair, stupid book."

Chris said "What a wonderful story. It shows that women can take initiative and be courageous and strong."

Alex danced around to carriage. "Yes, just like me!"

"Not like you, you couldn't rescue a flea. You're not strong enough," grumbled her brother.

"There is more than one type of strength." said Chris.

Chris, Alex and Ada all glared at Jo. He looked in the other direction and then asked "Could I go and get a drink?"

Alex chimed "I'll come too!" and chased him into the corridor.

Chris said to Jerome "Remember we were talking about creation myths earlier? I know another creation myth where it is a woman who creates the world. The Pelasgian creation myth: apparently it is one of the earliest known myths."

"Oh, really? I'm not familiar with that," said Jerome who liked to collect new myths.

"I heard about it on a radio programme about Women in Mythology.

"It's about Eurynome who created the world as an egg. She is a mother goddess of all things, and the whole world hatched from this egg. What I like about this story is that she danced the world into being, and she created such a wind that she could form it with her hands into a snake. The snake watched her dance and fell in love with her and coiled itself around the egg which contained the world. When the eggs hatched all the plants and animals came into the world. But of course the snake was male, and so he began to boast about

the world that he said he had created. So she kicked out his teeth and banished him from her world."

"Hah!" said Ada in satisfaction "What is it about snakes anyway?"

"Sorry?" blinked Jerome.

"Well, think of Adam and Eve. She got the rap in the Garden of Eden but really it was the snake's fault."

Jo came back into the carriage in time to hear this. "I would like a snake, they're so cool. One my friends breeds emerald tree boas."

Alex shrieked "Ewww!" while Chris suppressed a shudder.

Jerome said. "I suppose this story is also an example of an etiological animal tale, because it explains why snakes have so few teeth." He smiled. "Seen from another perspective this story shows us how mindsets can be maintained over centuries and millennia, and how stories transmit cultural values."

"I wonder how the story changed then, from the woman who kicked the snake to the woman who is tricked by the snake? That shows a big change in how society views women." Ada pointed out.

Jerome said "Stories can be positive as well as negative in perpetuating cultural values."

Inside Stories: A Narrative Journey

Eurynome, the mother goddess

Chris said "There you see the power of storytelling but also why students should be taught carefully to be aware of the reasons people have for telling stories, and the attitudes which might be hidden there."

Jo and Jerome discuss dyslexia

Jerome had noticed that Jo seemed upset. He caught up with him in the corridor where Jo was staring out of the window and scuffling his foot along the floor.

"Are you OK?" he asked.

Jo looked away.

"What's the matter?" said Jerome gently touching his shoulder.

Jo fiddled with the buttons on his PSP.

"Ahhh… it's so difficult. I feel so stupid. She's much younger than me and I can't even read properly. I'll never learn."

Jerome listened. "You're not stupid. You may just be good at different things. What do you like doing?"

Jo grasped his PSP and frowned. "I like playing on the computer. And sports. I'm good at that. I like to make things."

Jerome said "See—there are lots of things you're good at then. Is it just reading you don't like?"

Jo said "I can't concentrate in class. I get so fed up and sometimes I get mixed up when I can't remember all the instructions. My teacher says it's called dyslexia but I don't really know what that means. The other kids say it means I am stupid. The teacher said it means something else but I don't believe her. She *would* say that."

Jerome nodded. This was starting to make sense.

"My parents used to be upset because all the teachers were complaining about me. And then last term the psychologist teacher came to school and I did a test and she said it was dyslexia and now I get extra reading classes. But I have to go to other lessons and the other kids see me going out for extra help and that's when they say I'm stupid."

Jerome said "Did you know that there is a theory that some of the greatest geniuses were dyslexic?"

"Like who?"

"Well, Einstein for one (according to some people). What about Leonardo da Vinci? Some people say he was dyslexic too. Many people who are good artists find it difficult to spell but they have great imagination."

"What is imagination anyway?" Jo wanted to know.

"Imagination means that you are good at making up stories for instance."

"I can't make up stories because I can't spell." He was frustrated again.

Jerome "Have you ever tried just to tell a story and not write it?"

"No, you have to be able to write. That's what my teacher always asked me to do in school."

"Mmm. Well you could tell stories with animations like in cartoons or you could draw it in a comic strip. Have you never tried that?"

"Do you mean cartoons like Shrek?" he said, pointing to his PSP screen.

Jerome nodded.

"That's cool. Maybe I could do that. I've never tried." Jo brightened momentarily. "But I don't think so. I'm not good at anything."

Jerome said seriously "You must remember that dyslexia is an information processing difficulty. It isn't anything to do with how clever you are. And it's not your fault." Jerome's tone carried some authority. Jo remembered that Jerome was a professor. Maybe he did know something worth listening to.

"Jerome," he said suddenly. "Remember you were talking about the monkeys earlier? Can you explain that to me again? I thought that maybe I had too many monkeys or something.

Jerome was happy to explain. "People with dyslexia sometimes have problems with short term memory or visual disturbances. Think of it as if the monkeys are each carrying a chunk of information like a word or a letter. They are so playful that they don't stay in order, and they keep jumping over each other and losing track of their places. That makes it hard to remember information."

"Sometimes the letters do jump about on the page" said Jo. "They seem different every time I look at the page."

"Yes" said Jerome. "The monkeys may need to be trained. Special types of teachers can help you with that."

"I know, but it's so boring what I have to do. And if I don't do it my parents are worried I won't get a job."

"Don't worry. Lots of people with dyslexia do very well."

Jo wasn't quite convinced, but he was pleased to talk about it with someone who understood.

Not everyone likes stories

Back in the carriage a few hours later, the silence was broken by Chris' mobile ringing.

"Oh hello, Mrs Smith. I'm actually on the train just…"

"Oh yes, of course I remember who you are. Andrew is doing very well in the class now and he…"

"You mean our storytelling project? But it was so successful. The children enjoyed it and they said…"

Jerome looked up from his paper. Chris was sounding a bit agitated now.

"But really, Mrs Smith…I…"

Chris held the phone away from her ear and grimaced. Jerome could make out occasional phrases: "Disgraceful", "In my day…", "Waste of time. They should be writing essays."

After a while Chris gave up and cut across the diatribe. "Thank you so much for getting in touch. I'm sure we can discuss it more when I get back. I'm on my way to a conference on the future of learning."

As she hung up, there was an indignant squawk of "Conference? In my day we …"

"Oh dear," said Jerome, "That sounded awkward."

Chris was relieved to have a sympathetic ear.

"It really was terribly difficult," she agreed. "That was one of the parents from my class complaining again. Mrs Smith never seems happy with what her children are doing. Her latest complaint is our storytelling project. She says Andrew was upset because he had to listen to stories as if he was a baby and he didn't learn any proper writing last term."

Not everyone likes stories

Jerome was interested in this. "I would have thought that the pupils would enjoy listening to stories. What age is he?"

"Twelve, going on forty. Actually, most of the kids got a lot out of having the storyteller visit the class. He had them eating out of his hand! You should have seen their faces—they were just enthralled! But Andrew likes to think he is grown up and he wants to be a journalist. He didn't like making up stories and he thought it wasn't proper school work. The rest of them were off on flights of fancy, thinking up the most wonderful ideas, and I was so pleased with what they came up with. And all he could do was sit there and say 'I wanted to write a letter to the MP about the state of the school playing fields'."

"It sounds like he might not have had much previous experience of stories or at least not much beyond those that he remembers from his early childhood," said Jerome thoughtfully.

"Yes, it's interesting. I had a discussion in the buffet car with another teacher and the waitress. The teacher thought the children he was teaching were too old for stories and the waitress, who was a parent, was telling us about how much she and her children really enjoyed stories as part of their growing up. I think part of the problem is that parents are so anxious these days for their children to be able to pass exams, go to University and whatever. Then when we do work at school that does not seem to lead to some demonstrable outcome that ticks a box as far in the way that they understand, they think it is pointless. The newspapers don't always help much either with stories about how standards are falling or about children who can't reach the right standards in reading and writing. It is a real problem to get people to realise that being able to show that you have understood something or learnt something or developed in some way is not just all about being able to complete a test or pass an exam." Chris could feel that she was getting a little heated here and could see that Jerome was looking slightly surprised by her political enthusiasm.

The ticket inspector

Chris jumped as the door opened and a man in a newly pressed bilious yellow Trans-Europe express uniform walked in: "Tickets and Entry Profiles please, tickets and Entry Profiles ready please."

"We've bought tickets, but where do we get an Entry Profile?" asked Jerome.

"Health and Safety executive ruling, sir. We need to make sure that in case there is an emergency, people are able to embark and disembark without assistance. So you can't ride the train until you have learnt about how to get on and off. The Entry Profile stamp certifies that this is the case."

"But we're *on* the train, so it is obvious that we can get on, isn't it?" said Jerome tentatively, bewildered by the intrusion of this officialdom.

"Yes, but did you get on properly? I need to see evidence that you can get on *properly*," pressed the inspector.

"Well I can tell you *how* I got on—would that do?" tried Chris.

"No, the only way is for you to fill in this Entry Profile Assessment Exercise," insisted the inspector.

The ticket inspector

"We can replay the video that Jo took when we climbed on board," offered Alex.

"We could write you a poster so that other people know about Entry Profiles and tell them how to get on properly at the same time," offered Jo.

"But that is mixing up two objectives! Telling other people about entry profiles and learning about Entry are not the same thing," was the brusque response from the inspector.

Chris's mobile phone rang again—it was the parent who called earlier. She grimaced and was about to steel herself to answer.

"No mobile phones here I'm afraid. No mobile phones."

"Why?" asked Chris.

"That's our policy."

"*Why?*" asked Ada, looking up from her laptop and joining in the debate.

"We need to make sure that people concentrate on the ride and mobile phones interfere with the train technology."

"That's rubbish," said Ada, "and anyway, if people have their mobile phones they can tell other people about the ride too and they can look up information about the places we pass through and take photos..."

"All publicity and information about the Trans-Europe Express service must be authorised by the Trans-Europe Express executive. You might get things wrong."

"But how can a record of our personal experience of this trip be wrong?" Chris argued.

"This is stupid, I don't understand any of this," interjected Alex who had been adding some detail to the picture she had been drawing. Chris noticed that Alex had drawn a monster wearing a peaked cap just like the one worn by the Inspector. She was just about to cover this up with her handbag when Jerome said "Alex what is that the monster is wearing?"

Alex caught the Inspector's eye and said sheepishly "Errr, nothing…"

Jo thought quickly, "I don't know what all the fuss is about. At least we didn't come in through the window like the boy in the next carriage…"

The Inspector looked outraged, turned on his heels and marched out the door towards the next carriage, mumbling about "Violations of regulation 14a, sub-section 26, paragraph b1."

Ada returned to her work. Jo looked pleased with himself: he was used to helping Alex out of scrapes, but he thought that was a particularly good diversion. Alex added some fangs to the monster and coloured him a blinding shade of bilious yellow.

Jerome eyed Chris nervously, she looked quite scarily annoyed. At that moment, he had some sympathy with Alex and the rest of her class.

"See what I mean?" she exploded, "That's just typical of bureaucracy, all that form filling and what does it demonstrate? Nothing! Filling in that form does not have anything to do with actually getting on the train. We'll all manage to do that perfectly safely whether or not we fill in that form. I can understand that health and safety is important, especially with the train being so full and it being new, but there are other much more effective ways to help people understand what they might need to do in an emergency and why."

"You seem to feel strongly about it," observed Jerome.

She smiled ruefully. "Sorry. I do go on a bit. It's just so annoying when that happens at school. I mean, if the class have been working hard at storytelling, and I know their talking and listening skills have improved, and then someone comes along and tells me I should get them to fill in a worksheet assessing their storytelling skills. It might give evidence that they can *reflect* on their storytelling, but it doesn't give any evidence that they can *tell* stories. It's prioritizing the written word over the spoken word again."

"Terrible, terrible," agreed Jerome tactfully.

Jerome and Chris plan a study

"But I do worry about the underlying idea that education is like medicine." Jerome mused after a pause, "The methods used to see what has been learned often stem from the idea that a treatment has been given to a patient. As if reading books are the cure for the not-being-able-to-read disease."

Chris smiled at that. "Exactly," she said.

"Well, yes, but notice that medicine often has no real idea of why things work. For example, aspirin has recently been found to be effective at treating strokes. So we now treat stroke victims by giving them aspirins. Do we care how this works? Is this how we think of education? Don't worry about the *how* if the method works?"

Chris thought about this, and questioned "But if our reading books help children read then does it matter how this happens?"

"Maybe not, but I can't help feeling that the real change we want is not just more fluent reading but rather that children should obtain a love of reading amongst many other changes. How are we going to assess the full range of benefits?"

"You are not going to tell me to collect a hundred standardised tests to run on my children?" Chris sounded a bit worried.

Jerome said, laughing "No, no—that would be truly awful for the children and I don't think you would enjoy marking the tests either. I am thinking more of trying to engage with the children to find out what they are thinking and feeling—perhaps this might alert us to possibilities for improvement either in the way we work with the children or the materials we use. To do that, then you need to gather many varied sources of evidence."

"Like what?" asked Chris wearily. Sometimes it seemed to her that she spent all day collecting evidence of learning.

"Some testing can be useful to get an extra check on the progress of the children. For comparison, related data can also be collected from a similar class following the same curriculum."

Chris made a face.

"Alright Chris, I was going to say that talking with the children's teacher and the parents can give one extra insight." Jerome continued "And of course talking to the child herself: personal narratives are valuable to the researcher precisely because people emphasise the experiences which mean something to them."

"So you suggest looking much more at the learning experience in terms of the individual than at class progression?" Chris said,

Jerome and Chris plan a study

thinking of the ways in which government targets for class attainment would make this difficult to carry out.

"Yes, schools often become more like factories than I would like," Jerome said, thinking of the many discussions he and his colleagues had had with head-teachers, government inspectors, classroom teachers and parents.

"I would like to do some research in my class. I mean beyond the ticky-box forms I have to fill in. It would be great to have evidence that storytelling is effective," said Chris, "But I wouldn't know where to start."

"I can help you," said Jerome. "It would be interesting to run a study on this."

"Well it would be lovely if you could come and visit us." said Chris.

"Yes! And then you could see my pictures on the classroom wall," agreed Alex.

"Let's plan it now, shall we?" said Jerome, whose experience told him to strike while the iron was hot. "There are a few things we have to decide on."

He started a list in his notebook.

"First, we need to be clear on the purpose of the study and what research questions we want answered."

"I want to know whether stories help the children's English Language skills," said Chris.

"Mm-hmm," said Jerome, writing. "Which aspects exactly?"

"Their talking and listening skills."

"Good, good," said Jerome, "and when you say 'stories', do you mean children listening to stories told by someone else or telling their own?"

"Well it would be both, wouldn't it?" said Chris. "I usually get them to tell their stories to each other."

"Now we need to know how to operationalise "talking and listening skills." How would you normally measure that?"

"It's part of their curriculum assessment, so I would normally set them an exercise to do an informal presentation, and keep notes until I had covered the whole class. Listening is harder, so I tend to do it in smaller group discussions, perhaps after listening to a story or watching a film. Sometimes I work with my colleague in the next class and we help each other out. Sometimes when half the class goes to a specialist subject like PE or ICT or library, then I work with the remainder of the class because it's much easier with smaller numbers."

"When you do that, do you have criteria which you're looking for?"

"Kind of. It's a bit vague in the national curriculum documents. But you get a feel for it after a while, and I discuss it with my colleagues. We try to make sure we're being consistent but it's quite hard."

"That seems like a useful approach," said Jerome. "We should certainly consider how to evaluate these skills, and professional judgement from teachers has great validity."

"But the problem is that it's hard to run a class and watch the children properly to assess them. And it's hard to find a spot in the timetable when myself and a colleague can work together."

"Yes, I know that is hard," said Jerome. "If we could get a bit of funding for this, or support from your local authority, we could hire an expert teacher to work with you. Or pay for a substitute teacher to take your class while you observe. Of course, another option would be to have some of the researchers from my department who are experienced in observation to come along and work with you."

"It sounds very expensive," said Chris dubiously.

"It's sometimes necessary," said Jerome. "Research evaluation is very different from assessment as part of normal teaching. I've found in the past it's almost impossible to conduct the research study properly if you are trying to manage the class too. And it is hard to get good observational data from large numbers of children. It's just the way it is—if you are studying something in depth, it needs concentration and you can't fully focus on it if you are trying to run a class. Sometimes teachers find it strange to have such a high adult to child ratio in research studies, but then the aim is different. And it requires a different set of professional skills. But anyway, can you think of other teachers you might want to work with?"

"I think it would be good to work with other teachers in the local area. Then we could share good practice. Maybe we should get in touch with the local authority advisor for English Language."

"A good idea," said Jerome, noting it down. "Certainly we must get permission from the local authority and their support can be extremely helpful."

"We'll need to get permission from the head teacher too," said Chris, making a face.

"I can help with that," said Jerome reassuringly. "I know you've had problems in the past. It's usually easier if the local authority has given its blessing anyway."

"And permission from parents," said Chris.

Jerome added it to his list. "We'll give the parents information slips and consent forms for the children. I sometimes find it useful to put separate sections relating to consent to taking part, and to collecting different sorts of data. For example, if you have photo permission separate it can allow some parents to opt out of only that part whereas they might have previously opted out of the whole study if that was what was worrying them. We should also ask for the children's consent, but in words that they can understand."

"Do we need to disguise the children's names when we write about them?" asked Chris.

"That depends," said Jerome. "There are different schools of thought on that. My feeling is that if the children's creative work is quoted, they may wish to be identified as an author. But they may not wish to be reminded of what they said at 8 years old when they grow up, so you could use a pseudonym. In the past I have given parents and children the choice of whether to use their real name, and the choice of pseudonym if they prefer it."

"OK," said Chris. "That sounds fair. How long do you think we'll need to do this? And when?"

"You're better placed to answer those questions than I am," smiled Jerome. "How long do your storytelling projects normally last for?"

"Usually they would run for half a term or so. But we have another project in the first half of next term so that would clash. We could do it after that, though."

"That would be excellent," said Jerome. "That gives us time to plan it properly. We may need to defer it further if we can't get teacher cover arranged for you. Certainly it would take longer to

Jerome and Chris plan a study

arrange if we needed to apply for research funding. That can take a year or more, by which time everyone has forgotten what on earth they applied to do!"

"Would we need any special equipment?" asked Chris anxiously.

"We would probably record video and audio, but I am sure your school has a digital video camera. If not, I can lend you one. A laptop would also be useful for storing your notes."

"Now," continued Jerome. "Analysis. It can be very time consuming to analyse qualitative data."

"I can help," said Chris, "But I don't know what to do."

"We can train you. In fact, taking part in something like this and learning new skills is very important for your own professional development, so you must make sure you get recognition for it! Another thing we could do is team you up with a research student from my department. They would benefit from seeing good teaching practice, and you would benefit from the analysis skills they are developing[26]. Something to bear in mind is that transcribing discussions is very time consuming. We might need to find a little bit of money to get help with that.

"Well that seems like a good start," said Jerome, reading over his notes. "I can write this up into a plan and then we can make an appointment to see your head. You might want to talk to your local authority advisor informally in the meantime. Oh yes, and where do you want to publish this?"

Chris was doubtful "Oh, I couldn't possibly... I don't know..."

---

[26] For further information on analysis and research methods in general, see Cohen, L., L. Manion, et al. (2000). <u>Research methods in education</u>. London ; New York, RoutledgeFalmer..

"Of course you should tell other people about it!" said Jerome. "It would seem a pity to discover all these new aspects of storytelling and not share it with people. How about the other teachers in your school – would they want to know?"

"Oh yes, I wouldn't mind telling them."

"And the other schools in the local authority might want to know too. I could help you run a seminar if you want. We could write a case study article for an education web site, or even a paper for an academic conference."

"Really?" Chris said. "Oh that would be good. But frightening!"

"After all, you're showing your class work at the Future of Learning Festival this year," said Jerome. "So why not?"

"Don't remind me," said Chris. "I get butterflies in my stomach every time I think about it."

Good night

Chris was dreamily watching the lights of the town pass by from the train window.

Claire, the waitress she had met in the restaurant car, sat beside her for a moment taking a break from clearing the cups from the debris on the compartment table. "The town looks so peaceful at night, with all those flickering lights. It reminds me of the story of Godmother Death. You know, with all the flickering candles in the cave."

"I haven't heard that one."

Good night

Claire settled back in the seat. "It's one of my favourites, but I don't know why."

"Long ago and far away there was a poor merchant. When his wife had a baby he was delighted. But he was also worried about how he could provide for the child when they were already so poor. He decided that the best thing to do was to find a god parent for the child. But who? He thought long and he thought hard and he wandered here and he wandered there, trying to find someone who could give his son the best advantage in life. At the edge of the market place he came upon a shadowy figure who smiled at him from underneath her hood.

'I hear you're looking for a godmother for your son. I would be an excellent godmother.'

'Who are you?'

'I am Death.'

"The merchant was surprised but the more he thought about it, the more he thought it might be a good idea. After all, Death was powerful, and known by everyone. And of course, Death treated everyone equally. These would be good qualities in a godparent.

'I accept,' he said.

"Death did indeed prove to be a dutiful godparent. Every year she brought a present for her god son's birthday and made sure he wanted for nothing. When he grew up and decided to become a doctor, she knew she could help him further.

'When you are treating a patient,' she said, 'and the patient is gravely ill I will come to the bedside. If you see me standing at the head of the bed then the patient can recover and you should treat her. But if I stand at the foot of the bed, then the patient is mine and she cannot recover. You must not treat her in that case.'

"The godson was grateful to his godmother for her advice and carried out her instructions. He worked hard and gradually became known for his skill and compassion. When patients were very ill he would look to the figure of his godmother for help. If she stood at the head of the bed he would redouble his efforts to cure the patient, but if she appeared at the foot of the bed he knew that the best thing to do was to comfort the family and prepare them for what was to come. As his fame spread, he was eventually asked to become physician to the Emperor himself.

"One day the Emperor grew sick and weak. Nothing the doctor did would improve him although he tried all the potions and herbs known to him. With a sinking heart, he began to look for the familiar figure of his godmother. Sure enough, one day she did appear at the bedside, and to his horror she was standing at the foot of the bed. For the first time he faltered. He had grown to like the Emperor and did not want him to die. Furthermore, he was worried about what would happen to him if he did not cure the Emperor. So he put his head down and did not look at Death. He redoubled his efforts and managed to cure the Emperor, although he remained very weak. His Godmother vanished from the bedside, only to reappear later that evening.

'Godson,' she said sadly 'You have not kept to our agreement. It was the Emperor's time. He should have come with me. From now on you must heed me, or I cannot help you anymore.'

"The doctor was humbled and agreed not to go against his godmother in the future.

"As he stayed in the palace he got to know the Emperor's daughter who was very grateful to him for saving her father. She was as kind as she was beautiful and he loved her more as each day

Good night

passed. So he was distraught when he noticed that she was getting paler and thinner. She grew more and more tired and eventually took to her bed. Once again he tried everything he could to save her but again he saw the figure of his Godmother appear. He thought that his heart would break when he saw she was standing at the foot of the bed. He frantically searched his bag for more potions to try, for anything he could do, but when he glanced at Death, he was drawn by her gaze and became still.

'Must it be this way?' he asked.

'Yes, my son. Come with me and you will see.' The scene at the bedside seemed to shimmer and dissolve and he found himself in a vast underground cavern. It was lit by thousands of flickering glowing candles. As far as the eye could see in every direction, the candles stretched out to infinity.

'Each of these candles is a living soul. I light the candle when a person is born, and when the candle burns out, the person must die. This is the way it is and always has been. This is my appointed task.'

"She pointed to a small, guttering candle. 'This is your princess,' she said. 'In a few hours, her candle will burn out completely and I will come for her. There is nothing you can do apart from comfort her and tell her I will treat her kindly.'

Inside Stories: A Narrative Journey

Godmother Death

'But can I not save her? Can I not relight her candle?' He looked around wildly. 'Where's my candle? I could light hers with mine.' But even as he said it he knew this would not be possible. Death shook her head and they looked at each other for a long time. In that moment he understood that he should not try to change his Godmother's mind. She would come to everyone in time.

"The princess did die, and there was not a day that went by that he did not think of her until the day his Godmother came for him."

There was silence in the carriage, apart from the regular breathing of the sleeping children in the sleeping compartment.

Good night

The train rumbled on through the night. Chris wiped a tear from her cheek.

"What a lovely story," she said quietly. "What made you think of that story tonight?"

"I was at a funeral yesterday," said Claire. "An old aunt of mine. She used to crochet little ornaments for all her neighbours. That's the main thing I remember about her from my childhood. And somehow I think this is a comforting story. I like the idea that Death is such a gentle character. And that she's a lady."

Jerome said "I haven't heard that version of the story before, but I like it much better. The Brothers Grimm version is about Godfather Death and his Godson tries to trick him by turning the bed around, so that death is standing at the head. When Godfather death finds out that he has been tricked, he punishes his god son by mercilessly blowing out his candle. He doesn't seem to be so compassionate, but then this version is more about trying to cheat death. Which never seems to be a good idea in folk tales."

"An important message, though, that you should face death rather than outwit death," said Claire.

Chris said "You could use this story as a way to talk about a difficult topic. Stories can be quite good for helping children to get through difficult times. Especially when someone they love dies. There are lots of stories about that actually. In fact, there are very few fairytale parents who are still alive!"

Jerome said "What about the story where the mother is dead and comes to life again as a little bird who watches over her child and protects her from harm? She evens kills the evil stepmother by dropping a millstone on her head."

"Oh yes, and there's the one where the mother becomes a tree and is able to speak to her daughter and comfort her, and give her advice," put in Claire.

"It's an important theme, I would say," said Chris. "That when someone dies their love remains. " She paused. "When I think about it, that's part of the message of Harry Potter."

Claire thought about that. "I see what you mean. Harry has his scar, and even his blood is meant to still carry the protection from his mother."

Chris nodded. "There's even the bit in the last book where there is a folktale about Death."

"Don't tell me anymore," cried Claire "We haven't finished reading that one yet at home!"

"Oh, do you read before bedtime at home?"

"I read stories, but actually my daughter loves to tell *me* a night-time story, before she goes to sleep."

"What sorts of stories does she make up?" asked Jerome.

"All sorts of stories, sometimes about things that have happened to her during the day. In fact her hamster died a few months ago. She was so upset. She would tell me the same story about that hamster every night for a few weeks, but it seems to me that the story changed, as she learned to accept that Hammy was gone. It was as if telling the story had helped her come to terms with it."

"I had a little boy in my class who had lost his dad in an accident," said Chris. "It was so difficult to talk with him about it. But it was easier to talk with him about the characters in the story and their feelings. We worked with the Astrid Lindgren story about the Brothers Lionheart. First we read the story about the brother who loses his brother and keeps his relation to him in a different universe. It gave him lots of hope and helped cope with his feelings, and his classmates grew to understand him through their identification with characters in the story. Even for other emotional challenges, like a divorce or even just becoming a teenager and finding your way in life, stories can be a help. I suppose there is some safety in following the story through the eyes of a character instead of considering your own situation directly."

The adults talked quietly together for longer, until Claire and Chris had finished making the sleeping compartments ready for the night. They had to wake Ada, who had already fallen asleep over her laptop to persuade her to go to bed properly.

Chris switched off the light. "Good night," she said.

"Ayeeeeee!"

A scream broke the silence. Chris' heart was pounding—what on earth had happened to Alex? She turned on the light and went to the children's compartment.

"Alex," she said, "what's the matter?"

Alex was sitting bolt upright in her bunk. "Oh," she said, "There was a huge snake hiding in a plant, but it had eight legs and it had wings, and it was *horrible!*" she wailed.

Chris gave her a cuddle and stroked her hair. "There, there," she said resolving to give Jo a talking to for telling Alex scary things.

Jo, who was used to Alex's nightmares, had just grunted and gone back to sleep. Jerome had shuffled sleepily to the door of the compartment. "What was this?" he mumbled, "Did you have a bad dream?"

Alex was still terrified, but she was comforted to see Jerome's friendly white beard, and her breath slowed down again.

"What was it you were dreaming?" Jerome asked.

Alex started telling the dream again this time with more detail: "I dreamt I was walking down the corridor and suddenly there was a plant growing there, and in the plant there was a nasty green snake that was opening its mouth." Her lip quivered and she looked like she would cry again.

Jerome said "Now can you imagine the snake in front of you?"

Alex whimpered and Chris wondered what on earth Jerome was doing.

"Now when you can see it, just tell it to lie down."

Alex's expression started to change, and she was obviously concentrating. "It did it!" she exclaimed, "It's lying down now!"

"Good," Jerome said, "then you just ask it to be your friend."

"Friend?" said Chris.

"Yes," Jerome said patiently, "make it your friend."

Alex started to smile and looked much more at ease. In just a second she was back to sleep.

"See," whispered Jerome, "this is a tradition I once read about, that you should make friends with any enemy you encounter in your dreams. There is a small tribe that has been practicing this every morning for generations, and the children learn to face any danger or any threat they meet in their dreams through telling stories. It is remarkable that they have a very healthy society, with virtually no violence or crimes."

Chris yawned and put out the light again.

Good night

Technology to support storytelling

Sugar rush

Chris could see the warning signs. After a year of teaching Alex, she was alert to impending disturbances, like dogs are to earthquakes. She was wriggling around in her seat, chanting "Bored, bored, bored!" Jo looked only too ready for a distraction. "Ugly, ugly, ugly!" he chanted back. Chris looked at Jerome. She wondered what he would chant if he decided to join in: "Logico-scientific, logico-scientific, logico-scientific"? At present, however, he showed no signs of saying anything. He was asleep with his chin resting on his chest, his glasses halfway down his nose. From time to time he twitched and sighed. Perhaps he was dreaming of mermaids and ants. On the other side of the carriage Ada was stretching after a long stretch at the keyboard.

"About time too," Chris thought disapprovingly.

Alex was rootling around in the huge pile of sweetie wrappers and empty food cartons on the table. Somehow she and Jo had managed to consume three packets of chocolate chip cookies, four family size packs of crisps, a whole packet of mini mars bars and a litre of cola in the last thirty minutes alone. Chris had to admire their dedication. Their granny had obviously packed them an extra food bag for the journey. She had presumably meant it to supplement the healthy packed snacks which their father had prepared for the long journey, but they had taken it as an excuse to ignore their carrot sticks and hummus. All that sugar was probably bad news for the peace of the carriage, Chris reflected.

Sure enough, Alex accidentally-on-purpose kicked Jo and then flicked a balled-up chocolate wrapper at him.

"Oi!" he yelled, flicking it back. It ricocheted off Alex and hit Jerome's bow tie.

"One point for the bow tie, ten if you knock off his glasses!" shouted Alex.

Chris was momentarily distracted by Ada's sudden laugh.

"Don't encourage them!" she said sharply.

"Oh come on," said Ada, "Don't you remember how boring train journeys were when you were a kid? I once tried to dangle my brother out the window to see if I could get him to fly. It didn't work," she added regretfully.

Jo was now lining up chocolate wrapper ammunition while Alex fired them at Jerome. He shifted in his sleep, but didn't wake. "Grasshopper," he mumbled.

"Goal!" shouted Jo, as a ball of silver paper landed square on Jerome's glasses. "Ten points!"

Chris was sufficiently horrified by Ada's remark that she ignored the children for a moment. "How awful! Was he Ok? What age was your brother?"

Alex took advantage of the fact that Chris's disapproval was directed at someone else for a change. She had thought of a more direct way to hit the target. She scrambled up onto the seat beside Jerome and started stuffing chocolate wrappers in his ears.

"Twenty points for the ears!" Jo called out, with grudging admiration.

"Of course he was fine!" Ada laughed. "I used to dangle him out of the bedroom window at night so he was used to it."

"Oh," squawked Chris faintly.

Ada smiled reassuringly. "It's OK. He's a pilot now. It turned out pretty well for him."

Alex had now run out of sweety papers. Before Chris could stop her, she picked up Jerome's gold plated fountain pen and started scribbling on his face. She would normally have drawn a beard and glasses, but she was thwarted by the fact Jerome was already equipped with these. She opted for drawing a picture of a mermaid on his cheek instead.

Jerome's mermaid

"Whassamater?" blinked Jerome sleepily, then jerked awake. "Oh hello, Alex! Have you come to see me?" he beamed fondly.

She nodded and burrowed into his arm to hide her laughter. Jo suddenly realised that he was meant to be responsible for Alex.

"Alex," he said sternly, aiming for his mother's tone. "That was naughty. Look what you've done."

"I'll do it to you too!" shrieked his sister, bouncing across the carriage, pen in hand. Chris swiftly intercepted her and grabbed the pen.

"Sit down and behave, young lady. I'll talk to you later," she said treating Alex to her number ten grade teacher stare. Alex gulped and sat down again. Chris looked over at Jerome. He smiled back, oblivious, his new adornment curiously at odds with is otherwise dapper appearance. How was she going to raise the issue of a new tattoo to this distinguished professor? Now didn't seem a good time. She looked at Ada, who was surreptitiously taking a photo of Jerome with her mobile phone.

"You're no help," she snapped. "Now what are we going to do? We must find a nice game to play. Or maybe we could sing."

"Not singing," said Ada hurriedly. "You can play with my gadgets if you want."

Is technology anti-social?

"Don't you think there's such a thing as too much time with gadgets then?" Chris said tartly, still cross that Ada had been so little help. Not to mention her coming out with stories like the one about her brother. It might give Alex even wilder ideas the next time she had too much fizzy drink.

Ada smiled, a little nervously perhaps, and tried to sound conciliatory.

Is technology anti-social?

"I'm sorry. My laptop keeps me in touch with all sorts of people when I'm away."

Chris was still feeling irritable though.

"Yes, but don't you think all this technology can cut people off from normal social interaction? I certainly worry that some of my children are indoors shooting monsters in computer games when they could be playing games outdoors with each other."

"What's wrong with shooting monsters then?" Jo asked.

"Coz it's boring, stupid," Alex said grumpily, sliding a side glance at Chris to see if she was still in scary teacher mode.

"But a lot of them probably aren't killing monsters," Ada said firmly. "Lots of kids chat to each other in the evening using their home computers. That's social interaction, isn't it?"

"Chat systems can never be as good as real chat," Chris said, equally firmly.

"I can't go round my friend's house after tea though," Alex said. "It's too close to bedtime. But I can online chat."

"Yes, how do you think she learned to type?" Jo asked in a superior tone.

"My laptop keeps me in touch with lots of people I can't see everyday too," Ada added. "Just now I was on-line chatting to a friend who went to start some voluntary work in Kenya a week or two back. She's teaching in a primary school, and she was telling me what it's like. You might find this interesting too."

She passed her laptop to Chris, and Alex sat down next to Chris, craning her head towards the screen.

```
Jess: You there, Ads?
Ada: Hi. I'm on a train! How about you?
Jess: Internet café, nearest town.
Ada: How's things? You settled in now?
```

Inside Stories: A Narrative Journey

Jess: It's all beginning to seem a bit more doable now. You know I told you the school was built for 150 kids and we've got 600 now Kenya's made primary school free? Means we have to run the same lessons several times a day so they can do them in shifts.

Ada: Sounds like hard work

Jess: In some ways less work than back in dear old Manchester. These kids are so keen to learn! You wouldn't believe it—some of them walk ten kilometres to get here!

Ada: You mean they do twenty kilometres a day just to get educated? Well, not like being dropped off at the gate by your mum in a car I guess.

Jess. Yeah, a bit different. The jiggers are the biggest problem.

Ada: ??jiggers

Jess: Nasty little parasite beasties. Thing is, we've only got three classrooms, can't fit all the kids in even with shift teaching. So we do a lot of classes under the trees.

Ada: Sounds a lot nicer than a classroom.

Jess: Yeah, but there are jigger worms under the trees and the kids have bare feet. The jiggers burrow into their feet and lay eggs which hatch out later. Lots of foot infections, need the doctor—and you have to pay—time off school. Big problemo.

"Good grief," said Chris, when she read about the jigger worms.

"Eeurgh! That's disgusting," said Alex a few minutes later when she got to the same part.

"What is?" said Jo, sounding interested. He sat down on the other side of Chris to read the screen. "Oh my god', he said with emphasis as he read it. "Gross!"

Then he looked serious. "Makes you think though doesn't it? Walking twenty kilometres a day and jiggers in the feet just to do school. They must feel a lot different about it than I do."

Ada looked at Chris and grinned. "Something to be said for some gadgets then, Chris?"

Chris looked thoughtful but didn't say anything.

Making the invisible visible

Chris was deep in her own thoughts when the train jolted sharply.

"What was that?"

"Oh probably just leaves on the line," said Jerome smiling.

They all laughed.

"It's interesting how sometimes technology and nature don't work together isn't it?" remarked Jerome.

"That's true," agreed Ada "and yet technology can help us know so much more about nature too." she added pointedly.

"Thermometers and microscopes are technologies that have helped us understand a great deal about nature of course," said Jerome.

"Oh, come into the 21st century, Jerome! My car knows more about the weather than I do! What about GPS? What about the robots exploring Mars?" mocked Ada.

"I can think of a very nice example of children learning about nature through technology," said Chris. "I remember last year a teacher colleague of mine at the local secondary school was working with some researchers from the local University."

Ada tried to think who these researchers might be. [27]

"They were working on a project to provide a school field trip that was a bit different and the children had a great time as a result. They went on a field trip to the local woods, but when they got there the researchers had been there first and had added some things."

"What kind of things had they added?" enquired Jerome, tentatively, not wishing to reveal further ignorance.

"Well, for example the research team had set things up so that the children had different bits of kit..." Chris was unsure how to describe this and looked at Ada.

"What would you call them Ada, the children had..."

"Different devices?" offered Ada.

"Yes, that sounds right. The children were given different devices like PDAs and light and moisture sensors and there were also some screens and other sorts of technology in the wood that they could discover as they explored."

"So were they asked to explore particular things?" asked Jerome.

"Yes, I think pairs of children worked together and were asked to discover and hypothesize about the biological processes that were taking place in the wood," replied Chris.

---

[27] This section describes the Ambient Wood project. For more information see: Interact Lab. "Equator: Ambient Wood." Retrieved 29th May, 2008, from http://www.informatics.sussex.ac.uk/research/groups/interact/projects/Equator/ambient_wood-I.htm.

Making the invisible visible

"I suppose that would mean trying to find out about the different habitats for the plants and animals," suggested Jerome.

"So, when the children used these devices or they went into a particular part of the wood did they get added information that meant they could see or hear things through the technology that they could not have heard or seen without it?" asked Ada, who vaguely recalled a conference presentation about it

"Yes, that's what happened," agreed Chris.

"I think I see," said Jerome, still a little unsure.

"This new information was sometimes triggered by the children moving around and exploring and sometimes when they used certain devices," explained Chris.

"I know the project you mean," said Ada, "The technology digitally augments the environment. Some of the technology lets children take readings about the part of the environment they are in, such as how wet it is and other sorts of technology are triggered into action when the children move in a particular way."

"I still don't quite understand what the children would see or hear," said Jerome, puzzled.

"Well," said Chris, "I think that the children had a probe sort of device that enabled them to find out how wet a particular piece of ground was and how much light the plants living there would receive. The results were displayed on a little computer screen."

"I bet they were using GPS as well," added Ada. "That would mean that the children would be able to link the information they had collected about light and moisture with their position so that afterwards when they were back in the classroom they would be able to think about why one location might have been wetter or lighter than another."

"Oh, and another thing," added Chris, "There was a kind of periscope thing that the children could look through in the wood and they could see invisible things about the wood."

"What kinds of things?" asked Jo, whose interest has been stimulated by the mention of GPS.

"Small animals that might be living in that part of the wood, but that are too small to be seen with the naked eye, or little movies about the changes that take place in the wood at different times of year," explained Chris.

"I imagine that the children had an adult with them too to help explain things?" asked Jerome.

"Yes, I think that's true," Chris agreed, "They were also encouraged to think about what they had seen in a sort of den in the woods when they had finished exploring and to reflect on this and to discuss their findings with each other."

"So, in a way they were building a story about their experiences in order to try and understand more about the animals and plants in the wood. The technology helped them to build up richer stories because it made the invisible visible," Jerome speculated.

"Hmmm, that sounds great," said Ada. "Although it sounds like a lot of information for the children to pull together."

Jerome agreed "Yes, sometimes being realistic is the most important thing to help people understand and other times you need to lose some of the detail to help understand the most important things first."

"Sometimes it's good to look at slightly less realistic representations of the real world in order to understand the most important information," Ada jumped up and quickly produced a small magnifying glass from one of her many pockets.

"Here have a look here and I think I can show you what Jerome means."

She held the magnifying glass over her wrist and they realised that the glass part of the magnifier was in fact a small screen on which they could see the bones in Ada's wrist[28].

"Are they really your bones?" asked Alex peering closely.

"No," replied Ada, "They're simplified picture of the bones that are in a wrist."

Ada moved the magnifier on to Alex's knee and the screen changed to depict the structure of the knee bones.

"Is that my knee?" breathed Alex in awe.

"Gross!" said Jo. "You've got a knobbly skelly knee, Alex."

"No, it's like the wrist picture. It's a simplified version of a knee," explained Ada.

"The magnifier uses some clever computing to recognise the part of the body over which it is being held and then plays a movie of the structure of that part of the body on its screen," she expanded.

"Does it do animals as well as people?" asked Jo.

"No, this one is just the human body, but there is no reason why one could not be made for any animal as long as we know about that animal's body."

"Well, if it only does humans I'm surprised it recognises Alex's knee," said Jo grinning.

Alex stuck her tongue out at him and Jo smiled again.

---

[28] This device is fictitious. Sorry.

"In fact," continued Ada, "We can switch this knob here and then we can look at the blood flow, or the muscles."

"Ah, I see," said Jerome, "You can look at a simplified version of the body from different perspectives. That's very clever."

"Technology *is* very clever though isn't it?" commented Chris. "I know that at school the Head teacher is talking about us having some new computing technology that will help us personalise learning for each individual child."

"Well, the *people* who make technology are very clever, that's for sure," said Ada. "Technology is only as clever as the people who designed it. Or the people who use it, I suppose. There is a lot of work being done by people designing technology to make things that give each person who uses it an experience that is particularly suitable for what they need or want."

"Does that mean that I could have a little computer that was just for me and that would tell me about all the things I like?" queried Alex.

Introducing Bugsy

Ada opened one of her trouser pockets and pulled out a sleek, slim, shiny device. It was smaller than Jo's PSP, had only a couple of buttons on its edges and a touch sensitive screen that covered most of its front surface.

"I'll show you what I mean on myone." She gestured to the device.

Introducing Bugsy

"A what one?" queried a puzzled Jerome, peering at the myone in Ada's hand.

"This is a myone and I use it all the time for work. Or for fun. It's a bit like a window that lets me look at all the things I do in my life. I use it for almost anything from writing computer programs to storing the recipe for making my favourite guacamole."

Jerome considered all the things in his life and wondered what he would want a myone for.

"Alex—look! This is 'Bugsy'. He is my virtual pet dragon" continued Ada She showed Alex the screen of her myone and pointed to a small green dragon that was sleeping in the bottom right-hand corner of the screen.

"Shall we wake him up?"

Alex was curious about the sleeping dragon, but still a little in awe of Ada. She nodded her head vigorously. Ada stroked the dragon's back and tickled him under the chin with her little finger. The dragon woke up and cast a small fiery breath out over the screen. As the smoke from this disappeared Alex could see a message appearing on the screen where the smoke was. The message read:

"Hi Ada, how are you doing today? Did you enjoy your funk session at the 'Casablanca' the other night? I was enjoying a great dream about a knight, do you really want me to wake up?"

Ada smiled and said "Yes, come on Bugsy, time to get to up and meet my new friend Alex."

Alex looked pleased and smiled shyly as Ada turned the screen towards her and pointed to the small camera that is embedded into the top section of the screen on the myone.

"This little camera will pick up your image and then Bugsy can learn to recognise you as his friend," explained Ada, typing in the name 'Alex' beside her picture.

Alex was now a little more at ease. She gave a big smile at the camera.

"Hi there, Alex. I'm always pleased to meet a friend of Ada." Bugsy's gravelly voice emanated from the myone. Alex was captivated.

"What do you use it for?" she asked Ada.

"Well I have a very busy life so it makes sure I know where I have to be, when I need to be there and how I can get there. It knows all about buses, planes and taxis. Tell it where you want to go and it can give you the best ways to get there," said Ada with all the pride of a technophile.

"So it's a secretary?" asked Alex, a little disappointed. She thought dragons might do more exotic jobs.

"Excuse me!" said Ada indignantly, "It can do a lot more than that. I have loads of technology—you can see all those pockets I have. Most of them have some piece of kit in it. It helps me co-ordinate all the information about those bits of kit and all the stuff I discover when I am using them."

Chris had been listening to this conversation and was confused. "What exactly do you mean?" she asked Ada.

"Maybe an example will help," Ada suggested.

"In one of my pockets I have a camera, and in another I have a GPS tracker," she said.

"You are losing me already, I'm afraid. What's a GPS tracker?" asked Chris. Jerome nodded in agreement; he had no idea what a GPS tracker was either.

Introducing Bugsy

"Well, GPS stands for Global Positioning System, and this is a little tracker," she pulled a small yellow and black box that looked a little like a mobile phone from another trouser pocket and showed it to Jerome and Chris. Jo's ears had also pricked up, as one of his friends had been telling him about GPS and how it is used in cars to help people find a route from one place to another. He joined Ada, Chris and Jerome who were now huddled around the yellow and black GPS tracker.

Meanwhile Alex had the myone all to herself. Bugsy looked so lifelike that she half expected him to fly out of the screen. She imagined what he might say if he was real[29].

"Ada is very energetic so there's always lots to do. She can also be a bit bossy," confided Bugsy.

"Oooh, I know about bossy people. My teacher is here on this train too and she can be really bossy," said Alex in hushed tones.

"How old are you, Alex?"

"I'm 8 years and 1 week."

"Ah, so that means you are in Year 4. Do you know about food chains and webs? I know you learn about that in school when you are in Year 4."

"Yes I do. Those are fun."

"Have a go at this. It's a sort of game called the 'Ecolab' that helps you learn about them," suggested Bugsy.

Alex touched the Ecolab icon on the screen of myone. The screen changed, and Alex could see a picture of a pond, some trees, bushes and grass, with a big yellow sun in the sky overhead. A

---

[29] Bugsy is fictitious too, of course. The functionality which Ada discusses with Alex could be possible. It's possible for a device to be personalised to the preferences of its user. The sections where Alex talks to Bugsy are imaginary; devices which can understand and respond intelligently to human speech are far in the future.

message appeared on the screen inviting her to add some animals and plants to the world pictured on the screen[30].

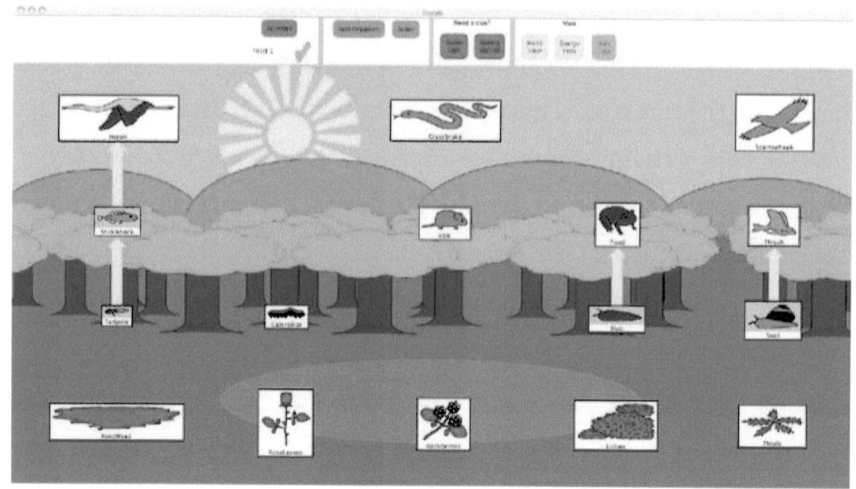

A screenshot of the Ecolab

While Alex played with the Ecolab on the myone, Ada continued her explanation about GPS to Jo, Jerome and Chris.

"This GPS tracker can communicate with satellites way up in the sky so that it can tell me exactly where I am on the earth. Look, let's switch it on and we can see." The screen of the device lit up and a picture of a small man appeared in the lower part of the screen. Then one by one a series of what looked like space ships appeared on the screen above his head followed by lines which joined the man to the spaceship.

"The man on the screen represents us, and the space ship looking things are the satellites that we are communicating with.

---

[30] Ecolab *is* real. You can download it for free here: . "Ecolab download." Retrieved 29th May, 2008, from http://www.riddles.sussex.ac.uk/Software/Ecolab/index.php, Ideas Lab. "Ecolab download." Retrieved 29th May, 2008, from http://www.riddles.sussex.ac.uk/Software/Ecolab/index.php.

Introducing Bugsy

When we have signals from a few of them, usually four, then the device can calculate our current position," explained Ada as the device flashed a message: 'tracking begun'.

"There," said Ada, "Now we can look to see what our position is." She clicked a button on the side of the device and a different screen appeared with some co-ordinates on it.

"See, we are at 47 18.360'N 5 01.83'E."

"OK," said Chris, "That seems very clever, but what has it got to do with the myone?"

"As I was saying I have a camera and I have this GPS tracker. When I go on trips I like to take pictures. My camera can record where I am when I take those pictures using the tracker. So, I have pictures on my camera and co-ordinates for where I have been on my GPS tracker," explained Ada.

Jerome and Chris nodded vaguely while Ada continued. "Then I transfer the pictures and the list of co-ordinates onto myone and I can link them to a map of the earth so that I can see the picture I have taken at the location on the earth where I took it."

Chris and Jerome still seemed a little puzzled about this, so Ada decided to show them. She asked Alex if she could have the myone back so that she can do this. Alex reluctantly passed it back and sank back onto her seat trying to work out how she might be able to get the myone back and talk more with Bugsy.

Imaginary friends

Alex had succeeded in retrieving Ada's myone. She had been sitting in the corner for some time, deep in conversation with Bugsy. Chris nudged Jerome.

"Oh look," she whispered. "Alex has an imaginary friend—she's talking away to him. Several of the children I teach do have pretend pals."

Jerome looked over at Alex. "You're right! Although Bugsy isn't completely imaginary because he does really appear on the screen. I think she's having imaginary chats with him though. I had a friend called Bob when I was a boy. He was always there when I needed someone to talk to, and I know that I found him a great comfort."

Chris wondered what Bob was like. Did he have a bowtie too? Did Jerome have a bowtie when he was a child? It was hard to imagine Jerome as a boy.

"I do know, though, that some parents worry about their children talking to people who are not there and wonder if this is a form of lying," said Jerome.

"Yes, it's true some parents do find this a cause for concern. I always tell them that it is a sign of a fertile imagination and that imagination is important for learning."

Jerome agreed with Chris, "There has been some recent research that has supported this view, Chris. It found that imaginary playmates can increase children's confidence and offer emotional support. There are even examples where the imaginary friend has helped a child talk about being bullied."[31]

"That's very useful to know," said Chris, pleased to have her intuitions confirmed. A question occurred to her.

"Do you think technology, like Jo's game machine and Ada's myone help children develop their imaginations or do they stifle them?"

"Hmmm," Jerome looked thoughtful. "Well, as you know, I am not an expert on technology but I don't think they stifle behaviour—they might change it, however. Even simple technologies can have a surprising effect on children's behaviour."

"Really, what kind of technology do you mean?"

"Well, take the humble telephone for example. Children who tell stories over the phone have been seen to produce more detailed and vivid stories than when telling them to someone's face."

"How odd! Why would that be?"

"Partly because the children are trying to make up for the fact that the phone can only convey their voice. The children added more context to their story telling, as if the phone encouraged them to add that detail in. Maybe when they were in the same room as the person they were telling the story to, they thought that somehow that person had more access to the details of the story in their imagination."[32]

"So, do you think that children have more imagination that adults, or do they lose some of this ability as they older? I know

---

[31] Taylor, M. (1999). Imaginary companions and the children who create them. New York ; Oxford, Oxford University Press.

[32] Cameron, C. A. a. W., M. (1999). "Frog, where are you? Children's narrative expression over the telephone. ." Discourse Processes **28**(3): 217-236.

that the younger children at school they love to play in the home corner and play different roles. As they get older of course they have less opportunity to play in that way, but does that mean they have less imagination?"

"These are hard questions that have vexed some of the great thinkers of our time," said Jerome solemnly. "There are some who believe that imaginative thinking is different to thinking about the real world, so that the activities that are involved in the imaginary thought are not really conscious."

"You mean like in dreams?" asked Chris.

"Yes, that's right. This means that the child cannot communicate these thoughts through their language, because language is part of conscious thought." [33]

"But that doesn't seem quite right. Imagination seems more active than that. What about playing games with other children? You know, make believe games. There they are communicating ideas from their imagination. And look at Alex. She's talking out loud to her imaginary friend."

"Yes," acknowledged Jerome. "I think you have a valid point and there are theorists who would agree with you." He stroked his chin gently, "It could be that imagination is, as you suggest, a much more active process that is linked to reality, to the child's developing thoughts and their language. A way in which children develop the ability to understand the world."

Chris felt happier with this "So that might mean that the child can develop their imagination just the same as they can develop their ability to understand maths?"

---

[33] For a readable introduction to Piaget's theory on this, see Boden, M. A. (1994). Piaget. London, Fontana.

"Yes," agreed Jerome, "the development of imagination would be linked to children's development of language skills and the people they interact with as they grow up – just like their other cognitive abilities."[34]

Personalisation

Whilst Chris and Jerome continued to discuss the importance of imagination, Ada chatted to Jo about GPS and SatNav.

Alex, who had become increasingly eager to get the myone out of the carriage, saw her chance. She waited until Jo and Ada were both looking at the SatNav screen, then picked up the myone and sneaked out of the carriage with it in her hand. She headed straight for the carriage where she knew some of the older school children taking part in the conference were based. She wanted to show off the myone.

"Are we going on an adventure?" asked Bugsy. "Shall I help?"

"How can you help me?" asked Alex.

"As I get to know you better and learn what you like, I can try and adapt myself so that I can offer you what you need. So for example, I think you like horses, so I can look out for horsy type stuff as we go along, or if I know you are learning about arrays in maths at school I can look for stuff about that too. Of course I can

---

[34] Vgotsky, L. S. (1991). "Imagination and Creativity." Soviet Psychology **29**(1): 73-88.

also help with finding our way around as I can access information about the train from the internet."

"Are there any horses on the train?"

"Not real ones no, but we are about to pass through Lipica. That's where they breed Lippizzaner, like those in this video clip."

Alex touched the video icon on the screen and a video clip of Lippizzaner ponies played. Alex squeaked in excitement and rushed into the carriage where the other children were congregated around a large pot of popcorn and a plate of cup cakes.

"Look, look my friend Bugsy has found this film of Lippizzaner ponies! They come from Lipica which is the next town we pass through on the train," shouted Alex excitedly.

The children turned round to watch. They all huddled round Alex and the myone as she introduced them to Bugsy. Alex enjoyed showing them some of the things Bugsy had shown her and being the centre of attention. She didn't notice that the inspector in the bilious yellow uniform had come into the carriage and was tapping his stamp machine against the door in an increasingly agitated manner.

"And what is this all about?" he exploded. "What on earth is that" he said, pointing an accusing finger at the myone in Alex's hand.

Alex turned round guiltily.

"It's my... I mean it's Ada's..."

"That device will be interfering with the train's technology, I demand that you give it to me immediately so that I can check its credentials and protocols."

At that very moment one of the smaller boys who had climbed onto the luggage rack in order to get a better view of the myone fell

Personalisation

off onto the table below. Cake and popcorn shot up in the air and showered down all over everyone. Alex took this opportunity to leave the carriage and head back to her own, using the myone to take a picture of the inspector who, had cup cake icing on his earlobe and popcorn in his hair on her way past.

Alex came back to the carriage breathless from her interaction with the Inspector and a little red in the face. She flopped down on the seat next to Ada with a huge sigh of relief. She then remembered that she had Ada's myone and looked up a little apprehensively to see the eyes of all the other members of the carriage staring at her intently. Accusingly, in the case of Chris.

"Eeermm. I just bumped into the Inspector, you know the one who wanted to see our entry profiles," she proffered as a distraction.

Feeling a little braver now she pulled out the myone to show them the photo she had taken of the Inspector with the icing in his ear in the school trip train carriage. As the picture appeared on the screen of the myone she saw that the inspector's head had now changed into that of a horse and that the cup cake was now a piece of carrot cake with a large orange carrot decoration embedded in the creamy white icing.

"But that's not what I took! It was the inspector!"

Bugsy appeared in the corner of the screen with big grin on his face. "I thought you'd like it, Alex."

"You've altered my preferences, haven't you?" says Ada suspiciously. "I like dragons, which is why Bugsy appears as a dragon and why there are dragon features added to some of my files. But you like horses and so the myone is changing to include more of the things you like. It's becoming personalised for you. I wonder what else has changed? Here, give me!" she said irritated and curious in equal measure.

"Hand it back, you naughty girl! How dare you..." said Chris, taking Alex aside for a row. She hadn't previously ever had to chastise a child for stealing someone else's digital dragon and turning it into a horse, but she felt she had to rise to the occasion.

Making games

"It's OK," said Ada. "Really, Chris. It's OK. I got it back and I've sorted it out so it's back to normal. She didn't do any harm."

Chris, who had been looking terribly worried for the last ten minutes, relaxed a little.

"It won't happen again, will it Alex?"

Alex shook her head.

"Because if it does," said Ada with a grin, "I'll get one of my friends from the robotics department to put a chip in your head so I can control you like a robot."

Alex looked doubtful, Jo impressed.

"Kidding!" said Ada hurriedly to Chris.

"Anyway," she continued, "You kids are driving me nuts. How about you borrow my laptop for a bit and find something interesting to do?"

"Oh that's a good idea!" said Chris. "You could write a nice story together."

Making games

"No way," said Ada, to Jo's relief. "Nah, let's do something interesting. How about you guys make a game?"

"Oh *Wow!*" said Alex.

"Could we really?" asked Jo. "A proper game with graphics and everything?"

"Yip!" said Alex. "Have a look here. And wipe your hands first. I don't want kid ectoplasm on my new laptop."

The children obeyed, rather in awe of Alex's giant, shiny laptop.

"Right," she said. "My friend showed me this a few months back. He's a real role-play geek. He loves acting out stories—you know all that table top stuff where grown men pretend to be elves and dwarves." She rolled her eyes. "At any rate, this game is called *Neverwinter Nights*. It's based on role-play rules, but it's not bad. The coolest thing about it is that you can make your own games using the toolset that you get free with it."

Alex and Jo crowded round to look at the screen. Ada selected the option to open the toolset and make a new game. "OK, so the first thing to do is make an area. That's like a level in the game. It'll be the first place that our player goes. You can choose. Do you want a forest? Or a dungeon?"

"Oooh! A castle!" said Alex reading the list.

"A sewer," read Jo with relish.

"No, a desert!" said Alex.

Ada selected the desert option. In a few clicks the screen changed to show a window containing a 3D picture of a desert divided into a grid of red squares. "Ok, this is the preview of what the desert will look like. You can move the camera around like this and zoom in and out like this."

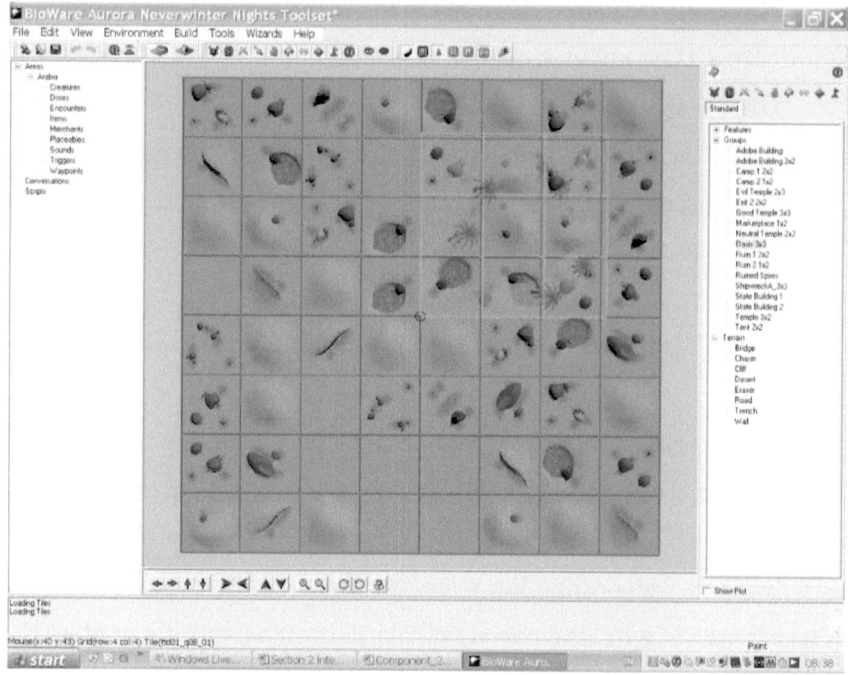

A screenshot of the Neverwinter Nights Toolset

"Cooooo-el," breathed Jo.

"But you probably want to add stuff in. If you click on this terrain menu here you can put in things like an oasis or a tent or a palm tree. There are hundreds of things you can decorate it with."

"Let me try! Let me try!" begged Alex.

Ada passed her the mouse. "Sure, just mess around and see what you can find out. And in a minute I'll show you how to play your game."

"A minute?" asked Jerome, who had assumed that making a game would be sufficiently complicated to keep the kids quiet for a good long time.

"Well, ten minutes," said Ada. "It's one of these bits of software where you can make something quite impressive in a simple way. A little input from the user has a big impact. But then you can get sucked in trying to improve it for hours. It's actually a bit like writing software in that things never work as you would expect the first time, so you have to keep iteratively tweaking it." She paused. "It's much more immediately satisfying than programming, though. The first thing I wrote when I taught myself how to program in Java was the classic 'hello world' program."

"What does that do?" asked Jo, looking up.

"It prints the words 'hello world' on the screen."

"Oh, excitement," said Jo sarcastically.

"That's what I thought! All that work and for what? Seriously, you do have to learn a lot of concepts in programming even to get that to work. Now students at my university are taught using higher-level programming environments so they can do more interesting things quickly."

"Zombies!" said Jo. He had been exploring the icons on the screen and had come across a list of characters. Chris looked over his shoulder. There was a long list of names of a bewildering variety of creatures. Jo started adding creatures to the world with gusto. "Aww …dragons! And skeleton warriors."

"Do be careful," said Chris anxiously "Don't break anything. And do you really need all of those characters? That seems like an awful lot."

Ada snorted. "Of course he can't break anything. He's just trying stuff out. You need to spend a while playing around to help you learn it. Wait till you see what happens when he plays it anyway."

"How do you play it?" said Alex. "I want to try it out."

"Just click on 'run game' from this menu.

Inside Stories: A Narrative Journey

The screen went dark and in a few seconds a welcome window was followed by a 3D scene of a desert. This time it filled the whole screen and there were no red grid squares.

Alex and Jo's game

"This is you," said Ada, pointing to a figure of a girl in the centre of the screen. When you want to move, just click the mouse where you want to go and she'll walk there."

"Most impressive," said Jerome who had moved round to have a look.

"There's my oasis!" said Alex.

"Doesn't the water look pretty?" admired Chris.

"What's that? Oh no! How do I attack? Oh no…" Jo exclaimed.

"That," said Ada with satisfaction, "is your skeleton warrior."

Making games

She watched Jo try to defend himself. "He doesn't seem to like you much, does he? Oops, and there's your dragon now. And zombies."

She laughed as Jo's character died in the centre of a colourful fight.

"That's not fair!" said Alex.

"Looks like you made your own game a bit hard for yourself. Here. I'll show you how to fix it."

She showed the children how to exit the game and return to the game-making toolset. "You'll find you have to keep doing this. You make something in the game and test it out, and then go back and make changes. Ok, now see all your characters in the desert. Some of them are hostile to the player."

"Oh, that's why they attacked!" said Jo.

"Yes, but you can change it here on the creature's properties. You can have hostile or commoners. Commoners are friendly, I think."

The children spent some time altering their characters before testing the game again.

"What happened to the parrot character I put in?" asked Alex. "It's not there anymore."

Ada looked at the other creatures engaged in battle round about. "Did you make him commoner or hostile?" she asked.

"Commoner. I wanted a goodie."

"Well it looks like he is surrounded by a lot of baddies." said Ada. "What do you think happened?"

"Maybe the hostiles attack the commoners as well as the player," suggested Jo. "Then my zombies probably killed the parrot before Alex got to that part of the desert."

"Could be," said Ada. "What are you going to do to fix it?"

"We could take the zombies out," said Alex.

"We could move the zombies further away from the parrot so they don't see it," countered Jo.

"Either sounds reasonable. Why not try and see if they work?" said Ada.

The children set to work, occasionally arguing with each other. But Jerome, who was listening closely realised that their arguments were of a different nature to their normal squabbles. They were reasoning about the behaviour of the characters within the game world and trying to infer the game rules.

"How interesting," said Jerome, "It's a bit like the scientific process."

"What do you mean?" asked Chris.

"The children are observing behaviour in the world—in this case a game world, but that doesn't matter—and they are thinking up explanations for that behaviour. They derive a hypothesis about the world, devise an experiment to test it when they change things in the toolset, and then carry out the experiment when they go back to the game world to try out their changes."

"I suppose they are," said Ada. "Isn't there an education guy who writes about how games help learning? I'm sure I remember hearing something like what you just said before."

"There are several. James Paul Gee and Marc Prensky are commonly known. I've never paid much attention to that part of my field before, because I'm not really interested in technology. But *this*... this is interesting," he said, watching in fascination as Alex and Jo earnestly discussed the sight radius of zombies.

Making games

"James Paul Gee is a respected academic who formerly wrote about linguistics. He has written a couple of books recently about what education in general can learn from video game designers." Jerome shook his head in perplexity, as if wondering why a linguist would turn to the dark side. "I recall a colleague telling me that Gee's argument is that video games are well designed learning experiences in the sense that they have to teach a very wide range of players how to play the game and keep them interested and challenged. Different players have different interests and ability levels but he argues that games are good at tailoring to individual's needs." [35]

"Well, they have to be, or people will stop playing and then tell their friends not to buy it," said Ada.

"Quite. Whereas education is in the privileged position that children are legally compelled to be educated whether or not they are satisfied with their experience of learning. Anyway, Gee also developed an argument along the lines that as people play games, they are going through the process of hypothesis testing – seeing the behaviour of the game world, forming explanations for it, and changing their actions in the game to test their hypotheses. But what Alex and Jo are doing just now is more powerful because have much more control about what happens in the game because they made it in the first place. They can go outside the game world, into the toolset and see what happens behind the scenes."

"Can I talk to my guys?" asked Alex.

"You mean conversations? Yes, that's fun! I'll show you."

---

[35] Gee, J. P. (2003). <u>What video games have to teach us about learning and literacy</u>. New York ; Basingstoke, Palgrave Macmillan. Learning Principle 11.

Alex watched as Ada brought up a new screen called a conversation editor.

"In these game conversations the player gets a choice about what to say. So you have to think of the possible things the player might want to say and write them in advance. We start with what the game character says. Who do you want to talk to?"

"The parrot!" said Alex. "Make him say 'Pretty Polly!'"

Ada typed in the text, and the line of dialogue appeared in red on the screen. "Now, the blue lines are going to be choices that the player could say. What's one possible thing the player could say when the parrot says Pretty Polly?"

"Where did you learn to talk?" said Jo.

"You're not so pretty really," said Alex.

"OK, OK," laughed Ada. "That's two choices already." She typed them in and the children saw two blue lines appear under the parrot's red line. "Now what would the parrot say if the player picked 'Where did you learn to talk'"?

"Ummm. From a sailor," said Jo. "He taught me some good swear words."

"OK," said Ada, typing that but deciding to move on before Jo gave any examples to horrify Chris. "And what would the parrot say if the player said he wasn't pretty?"

"He would say 'don't be rude!' Make him say he has lovely red and green feathers!"

As Ada typed the structure of the conversation became clearer. "You can have as many back and forth turns between the player and the parrot as you want, so the conversation could go on forever. And you can have as many choices as you want."

Making games

She decided to exact a minor revenge on Jerome. "In computer science terms," she said gravely, "This is a tree. The depth of the tree is the length of the conversation and the breadth the number of choices. Every time the player makes a choice, that's a branch. And the lines which end the conversation are leafs in the tree."

"Isn't that upside down?" asked Chris.

"Computer science trees are always upside down," Ada explained.

Alex and Jo were testing the conversation in their game. When they clicked on the parrot, the conversation text appeared at the top left of the screen. They could select between the options they had previously specified and follow the conversation down one path of the tree.

A screen shot of the conversation with the parrot in the toolset

Inside Stories: A Narrative Journey

A screenshot of the parrot talking to the player

"Is it possible to make the parrot do something when the player is rude?" asked Jo.

"Good question," said Ada. "Yes, you can make him attack the player or fly away or something. I'll show you."

After she had demonstrated to the children, she commented to Jerome "Every node in the tree—every dialogue line, that is—can have a script executed from it. It means you can set up consequences for things the player says."

"Can you do other things as well as attacking?" asked Chris. "It all seems so violent."

"Yeah, you can give the player a present, or tell him some new information or put him further forward in the quest. You can put entries in the player's journal to tell him what he has to do in the quest. You can make the quest quite long and complicated if you want, or you could start with a simple one, like "Rescue the prince and I will give you a dress that is not a paper bag—like a new version of your story!"

Chris laughed.

"How do I make it so that the parrot says something different the second time I talk to him?" asked Jo.

"Another good question," said Ada. "I'll make a computer scientist of you yet. What you need to do is set up conditions on dialogue lines. It's like making the computer check to see whether something is true, or whether something has happened before it makes the character say the next line. You can check to see whether the player is a boy or a girl, or whether it is morning or night-time. Or, more usefully, what the player is carrying or whether the player has had this conversation before. Or even, if you have been keeping the player's journal up to date, you can check to see what part of the quest they have already done."

"That's interesting," said Chris. "It's a bit like those 'Choose your own Adventure' books, isn't it? You know: 'if you want to explore the cave, turn to page 63. If you want to run away turn to page 31'. And so on. And sometimes it only works if you have already collected something, like a rope to lower yourself into the cave."

"Exactly," said Ada. She showed the children how to use the interface to set up conditions. Jerome, watching over her shoulder, was at a loss to keep up with her instructions. But he also noticed that the children appeared to have fewer problems than he did.

"They seem to understand it conceptually," he thought. "And their visual memories seem excellent. They're able to remember where to find the most obscure options."

He asked Ada about it. "Well, I don't think the interface is particularly well designed," Ada said. "They could have done a better job in making it easy for people to remember where to find features. But still, the kids are doing fine."

"They are getting on much better than me!" said Chris enviously. "I would be nervous using a program like that."

"Well the kids are just used to it," said Ada. "They've been using software for years and they know the conventions."

"OK," she said to the kids. "I'm going to get some coffee. Don't get ectoplasm on my keyboard."

Chris's heart sank. She felt sure that the kids would ask her all kinds of questions which she wouldn't be able to answer now that Ada had gone. It turned out that her fears were unfounded. The most difficult question they posed was how to spell "ectoplasm."

"The game's going to be about a haunted house!" said Alex excitedly. "And someone has to go and find out the mystery."

"Yeah! It'll be great," said Jo, smiling at his sister.

"Well well," thought Chris. "Wonders will never cease."

Jerome is jumped by zombies

"Do you want to play our game?" Alex asked Jerome.

"Oh well... I..."

"Come on," said Alex, "It's great!"

"Yeah, have a go," said Jo. "Please?"

Jerome is jumped by zombies

"What a nice idea," said Chris, hoping to delay the inevitable moment when she must play.

Jerome took his courage in both hands. "Show me what to do" he said.

"It's easy," said Alex. "You just point here and click and then your character goes walking to where you want."

"Marvellous," said Jerome, peering over the top of his glasses at the screen. He carefully moved the mouse and watched his character move in response. "Oh look, I seem to be some sort of elf lady!"

"Go over there!" said Alex pointing on the screen. "Go there to my haunted house!"

"Don't tell him that yet! It's meant to be a secret!" cautioned Jo.

Jerome moved slowly across the desert scene. He met a parrot on the way and stopped to talk, laughing at the conversation.

"Pick to say he's not so pretty," chortled Alex.

Jerome, unsuspecting, selected that dialogue option with the result that the parrot attacked his character.

"Fight!" said Jo. "Quick, equip your dagger!"

"Do what?" said Jerome in confusion.

"Click on this one," pointed Jo. Jerome did so and watched his character fight the parrot.

"Oh well, I won that one," he said. "Seems a shame though. Couldn't I just have run away?"

He continued through the level. Unexpectedly three zombies appeared at the intersection of a path, groaning in an unfriendly fashion.

"Ha!" said Jo with satisfaction. "My encounter point."

"But where did they come from?" asked Jerome in alarm. "I didn't have any warning." He equipped his dagger and started to fight as he had be shown, but quickly found that he was no match for three zombies at once. His character sank to the ground and a dialogue box appeared giving him the option to 'respawn'. He clicked on it, and his character came back to life. He did this several times in a row, until Jo took pity on him.

"Let's try the level inside the house instead," he said.

"Yes please," said Jerome gratefully. "It will seem quite peaceful by comparison."

As Jo loaded the haunted house level, Ada came back with her coffee.

"How are you getting on, Jerome?" she asked in amusement.

"He got killed by all those zombies from my encounter point," said Jo.

"No wonder," said Ada. "What's he playing as? An elf wizard? He's got no strength for fights like that."

"I have a dagger," said Jerome with dignity.

"You'd be better off casting spells if you're a wizard. Anyway, Jo, did you give him any warning about that encounter?"

"No," said Jerome. "Those zombies came from nowhere. One minute I was strolling through the oasis and the next I was set upon by zombie hordes."

"It was horrible," agreed Chris, tongue in cheek.

"Mmmm," said Ada "That's a bit unfair, having an encounter point like that without a warning like bones strewn around the path on the way there. That would give the player some chance of preparing for it, or avoiding it."

"I suppose so," said Jo, torn between objections to the criticism of his encounter and bloodthirstiness for a path strewn with bones.

"Look, here's the haunted house level loaded now!" said Alex. "Go here!"

Jerome took the mouse again and navigated through the house.

"There! Go there! No, not there, stupid!" said Alex, pawing at the screen.

"Alex!" said Chris.

"Oi!" said Ada "Get your fingers off my laptop screen! When someone is testing your game you have to bite your tongue and not keep telling what to do and where to go. If you keep quiet and watch them you'll see where they look confused. That's a place where you might need to work on it to make it more obvious for them. You can ask them what they were thinking about afterwards. It's like when you work in a shop you would have to think to yourself 'the customer is always right', no matter how annoying they are. When someone is playing your game, you have to say to yourself 'The player is always right.' No matter how dim they might be," she said watching Jerome's painstaking progress.

"I think he's doing very well," said Chris.

Jerome came across a glowing green slime trail.

"Ectoplasm," said Alex proudly.

"Arrg!" said Jerome as he was beset by a series of wraiths.

"Good," said Ada. "You warned him that time with the ectoplasm."

"Ah," she added a moment later. "You got the balancing wrong there."

"What do you mean?" asked Jo, who wanted to know more about these technical terms.

"Fairness, really. If a game is balanced it's not too hard or too easy for the player. It's set up so the player has some chance at succeeding and the odds aren't stacked against him. There you've got six wraiths against one beginner level wizard and he has no chance at all."

Sure enough, Jerome's character died and he had to respawn repeatedly until Jo showed him how to quit.

"Think of it as if you were in a fight. You wouldn't think it was fair if you were jumped by six big guys at once. You have no hope. But it's OK to do it in the game if you give the player a chance, maybe by giving them a weapon they could use, or some armour, or even giving them an invisibility cloak to sneak past."

"Did you like it? Did you like it?" asked Alex excitedly.

"Yes, very much," said Jerome settling back into his seat once more. "I liked your parrot and I thought the desert was lovely. But I didn't quite understand what the parrot had to do with the haunted house."

"Why don't you ask Jerome what you could do to make your game better?" prompted Chris.

"Give us 3 stars and a wish," said Alex. "Like in school."

"Three stars and a ...? Oh I see..." said Jerome. "Three stars: I liked all the decorations you put in the setting, I thought the conversations were funny and I liked the haunted house idea. And for a wish: I wish there was more of a storyline."

"What do you mean?" asked Alex.

"Well I found it a bit confusing. I didn't know what I was meant to be doing in the desert or the haunted house. I would have liked it if I had a mission or quest to carry out. I would really have liked to know why those ghosts were there. What did they die of?"

Alex and Jo looked at each other.

"I dunno," said Jo. "They were just ghosts."

"But what if your mission was to find out how they died so they could be put to rest?" asked Ada. "That would be cool."

"OK," said Alex. "Jerome, you help us!"

Filling in the gaps

"Oh dear…" said Jerome, "Let me think about that for a bit."

The children continued working on their game while Jerome searched through his newspaper.

"I know it's here somewhere," he muttered. "Aha!" he exclaimed, folding back a page and smoothing it out.

"Ancient Bones Found on New Building Site," he read. "Development on an estate of new houses in the Midlands was suspended yesterday as builders discovered human bones in the rubble of the demolition site."

"Oooh!" Alex sighed with pleasure.

"A police spokesperson said that the pathologist confirmed the bones were human, but were from not one but *two* separate skeletons. The bones are believed to be at least one hundred years old. The investigation continues."

"But what happened?" asked Chris.

"It doesn't say," said Jerome, "But we could fill in the gaps by making a story."

"The ghosts in our game could be the skeletons they found when they demolished the old house."

"It still doesn't answer why the people died," said Ada thoughtfully. "Did it say anything about that?"

"No," said Jerome.

"Hang on a minute then," said Ada. She turned on myone and connected to the web. "Ah. OK. Your newspaper was the morning edition, Jerome. I've got a more up to date report online. Right… hmmm… the pathologist reported that the cause of death was unknown. There were no marks on the bones or the skull."

"Well, those poor people were found when the old house was knocked down," said Chris. "Maybe they were buried under the floor, or walled up in a room! I went to Glamis Castle in Scotland and there is a room which was walled up and sealed off hundreds of years ago. You can see where the window was bricked over on the outside of the building. The guide said it was because the Laird and his friends played cards on the Sabbath and the devil came to play cards with them. The devil bricked them up inside the room, and they're still playing to this day."

"I bet they were murdered," said Jo gleefully. "I bet someone did them in and buried them under the floor and no-one ever knew."

"Maybe they were killed without a struggle. No marks were found," said Ada.

"Poisoned," said Alex.

"I can't imagine anyone wanting to buy a house on that site now," said Chris.

Filling in the gaps

"I don't know," said Ada. "Increases the market value, doesn't it? Buy a house, get a ghost free. In fact buy one house, get *two* ghosts free!"

"I think the skeletons were a man and a lady," said Alex. "and they wanted to get married, but another man was jealous so he poisoned them and hid them under the floor."

"But wouldn't people notice if two people went missing like that? No, they would suspect the jealous guy," objected Jo.

"Not if no-one knew that they were in love," said Alex.

Jo looked revolted by the romance. "I know!" he said. "How about: they were strangers to the town and they made the mistake of going to the mad axe-man's inn to stay the night? He killed them and no-one missed them because they were strangers. And and... he chopped them up and fed their meat to the other guests!"

"Yuck!" said Chris. "Wouldn't the bones have been in a bit of a mess if that happened? It's like those awful stories you get on tours in Edinburgh about the family of cannibals and Burke and Hare. They're a blood thirsty lot, the Scots."

"Why don't you go with Alex's idea with the couple who were poisoned?" said Ada. "We could put a flashback in the game where they ghosts show you what happened, but only if you find enough clues first."

"Maybe you have to find the poison bottle and when you touch it the ghosts appear and tell you about it!" said Alex.

"And before that you keep seeing the ghosts out of the corner of your eye, and hearing ghostly noises and blood stains and lots of scary stuff like that!" said Jo.

"Now that sounds like a game I would like to play." said Jerome. "The suspense will be most satisfying."

How realistic should a game be?

Ada spent some time working with the children on the more complicated aspects of their game. They were easily able to place blood stains on the floor and write ghoulish conversations, but it turned out to be more difficult to make events happen depending on where the user went in the house. She showed them that every object in the game world could have a set of scripts which would be triggered under particular circumstances.

"If we wanted it so that a ghost appears when you pick up a bottle, then we'd need to put a script on the 'on use' script slot for the bottle."

"Do you mean a script like in a play?" asked Chris.

"No, it's an overloaded term here. I mean a mini computer program and you mean lines of dialogue, and stage directions I guess. It's more like the stage directions—it's a series of events which will happen once the script has been triggered."

"Make it so one of the ghosts comes and talks to you and there's a thunder clap and then it calls the other ghost over but only if you're nice to him." said Alex.

"Hang on!" said Ada indignantly "I'm not your code monkey! These things take time you know."

Alex giggled and made monkey noises in Ada's ear.

"Oh for heaven's sake!" said Ada. "Give me peace. Go and draw a monkey typing or something for a bit."

Jerome could see why Ada needed to concentrate. He looked at the screen where she was typing lines of code in a computer program. She was explaining what she was doing to Jo as she did it, and he was nodding valiantly.

How realistic should a game be?

"Now test it," said Ada "It might not work first time, though."

Jerome asked her "That part of the game making toolset seems much more complicated than the rest of it. Wouldn't you agree?"

"It is. It's a pity actually, because to make your game interesting you need dynamic behaviour which usually needs a bit of scripting. It's perfectly easy if you know how to program…"

"…Which most eight year olds don't," said Chris.

"Sure, but both Alex and Jo understand the underlying logic of what needs to happen. If the interface was better, then they could manage the scripting themselves. There are visual programming languages for children where it's not typing difficult syntax but dragging and dropping instead. It wouldn't be too hard to write a visual language for this." Ada said thoughtfully. [36]

"It didn't work," said Jo in disgust.

"Hmmph," said Ada. "What happened exactly?"

Jo explained. Ada and he started to debate what might have caused the problem and they went back to look at the script.

"I could never help him with that," thought Chris.

"This always happens," said Ada reassuringly to Jo. "It's just part of programming. No one says you need to get it right first time. Or even the second time. You just have to be patient and unravel the knots one at a time."

---

[36] In fact, the Adventure Author and Script Cards projects at Heriot-Watt and Sussex Universities aim to make *Neverwinter Nights* easier to use in classrooms and include simplified scripting for exactly the reason Ada mentions. See www.adventureauthor.org and Katherine, H., G. Judith, et al. (2007). A learner-centred design approach to developing a visual language for interactive storytelling. Proceedings of the 6th international conference on Interaction design and children. Aalborg, Denmark, ACM.

"A good lesson in general," said Jerome, pleased that Ada was taking the time to support Jo in this difficult task.

Alex left her drawing and came to watch the screen as they tested the game.

"It's not very realistic," she said critically.

"What isn't?" said Jo absently.

"The house. When you look at it from the outside then the roof fades away and you can see inside the walls."

"Yeah, some games are like that," said Ada. "It's just the way the game engine works. You switch between camera views to get a better view of things. It's to make it easier for the person playing it."

"Well that's not very realistic either," Jo pointed out. "You can't just change your camera angle when you're walking down the street in real life."

"And you can't just barge into people's houses without ringing the doorbell either. And people don't hang around waiting to talk to you in real life," said Ada. "They're just game conventions. Some of them are pretty stupid, I agree, but players just accept things like that as what happens in games."

Alex still wasn't happy. "Wouldn't the blood stains dry up so the player couldn't see them? And the player has been walking around for ages, so she'd be hungry in real life. We should make it so you can have sandwiches in the game."

Chris took the hint. She could see Alex was getting fractious as she regularly did when she was hungry. She unpacked one of the picnic bags and handed round some sausage rolls.

"I don't think we need to have a meal for the player in the game," she said to Alex. "It would get a bit boring for the person who was playing it. They would want to get on with the mystery instead of sitting down for a picnic!"

"It's the difference between real life and drama," said Jerome. "In a story, or a play or a game in this case, you're not trying to recreate real life in every mundane detail. Often the purpose is to make a moral point, or to study an emotional behaviour or reveal an insight into the human condition. Emotional veracity is the important aspect in drama."

"What?" said Jo. "Again the with dictionary swallowing, Jerome!"

Jerome looked sheepish. "I mean that it doesn't matter that you are true to every routine of everyday life, only that you give a flavour of what life would have been like to a person in the situation you are trying to represent. What is really important, though, is that the motivations of the character seem real to the audience, that they understand why the characters do what they do and that their relationships seem plausible. You could think of drama as a search light which picks out shades of human emotions, but doesn't focus on the routines of everyday life."

"After all," said Chris. "You can go and wash your dishes anytime you want. You don't need to see your character doing it!"

Ada laughed. "That always bugged me about the Sims. If I want to tidy up pizza boxes and look up the newspaper to find people jobs, I can do it in real life for my flatmate. So it's more fun to make them do the crazy stuff in the game."

Alex perked up "I'd rather eat a real sausage roll than watch my character do it in the game. And we could say that the bloodstains on the floor are magic and can't be wiped up. That's why they have been there so long."

"That's the spirit," said Chris. "Now why don't you finish up your lunch and go and wash your hands so you can use Ada's laptop again? Come on," she said to both the children. "Go and get cleaned up."

When the children left, Jerome said to Ada. "That was nice of you to work with Jo there. He really enjoyed working with someone who took him seriously."

Ada looked surprised. "Why would I not?" she said. "He's a bright kid."

"Really?" said Chris.

"Oh yeah... he was very quick to pick up programming. I wish the students in my lab classes were all that quick."

"It will do Jo good to realise he is good at something," said Jerome. "Particularly as it has such a high cultural value for him."

"Eh?" said Ada.

"Making games is ...err.. cool, I believe you would say."

The digital divide

Alex looked out of the train carriage and saw that they were pulling into a station. She was sure that there was not a scheduled stop due and so she was surprised when the train drew to a halt. She read the station sign 'Lipica' and her boredom turned to excitement as she remembered the video of the beautiful Lippizzaner ponies she had seen in the video clip on the myone.

The digital divide

"Are we stopping?" asked Jerome blearily as he woke up from a doze

"Yes," said Ada

"We're not scheduled to stop here, but we seem to be at Lipicaner."

"Yes," said Alex, keen to show off her new knowledge about this place "It's the home of the famous Lippizzaner ponies that are known for their beauty and agility all over the world"

The rest of the carriage turned to look at Alex, impressed by her statement. All except Jo of course who turned his eyes to the sky and muttered "Typical! Horsey, horsey Alex."

"Apologies, Ladies and Gents, we are making a short stop at Lipica to pick up some fresh food supplies. We will be here for 30 minutes and you are welcome to leave the train and stretch your legs on the station," said a nasal announcer over the speaker system.

"Oooh please, please can we go and see if we can find some Lippizzaner?" squealed Alex jumping from one foot to the other.

"Ok, I'll come with you," said Jerome, smiling at her enthusiasm, and keen to get a breath of fresh air himself.

"How about we go and see if there is a station café, Jo?" suggested Ada "We could have another go with the GPS tracker."

Chris decided to stay put and take advantage of a little peace and quiet.

Ada and Jo headed off towards what they thought was a café at the end of the platform. "Look there's a sign with a picture of a glass on it," spotted Ada "Let's head that way and take a look."

As they drew near they realised that the building was a workshop. Peering inside, they saw a group of men and women packing glasses into boxes. The glasses were exotic colours and shapes and the whole inside of the building was bathed in a rainbow of glittering light. As they turned to their left they saw a tall man blowing through a tube, which he was turning in circular movements. As he blew, a magnificent scarlet bubble of glass expanded and caught the light from a nearby fire. Ada pulled out her myone to snap a quick video clip to show the others when they got back.

Jo shrugged his shoulders "What's so interesting about a load of glass? If you go down our high street there are loads of shops and I bet some of them sell glasses, but would you want to take a picture of them?"

Ada was about to protest the virtues of craftsmen such as these when she realised that she and Jo had been joined by a small boy.

"Hello," said Ada "what's your name?"

"I'm Mark and that's my dad you are watching. What's that in your hand?"

Ada turned to show Mark the myone and explained "It's a small computer with a video camera. I was going to take a short clip of your father blowing the glass so that I can show our friends when we get back on the train."

"I've never seen a computer like that before!" exclaimed Mark. "We have a computer in our classroom at school, but it's a lot bigger than this. It doesn't take pictures either. We use it for writing and sometimes we play a game about a maze where you have to solve maths problems to find treasure."

"I play games too. Have you got a PSP? I like playing shooter games with blood and gore, sometimes role-playing ones too,"

The digital divide

asked Jo sensing that there might be an unexpectedly kindred spirit here and a chance for a quick game of KnightCastle or Vader.

Mark looked puzzled and then a little awed "Do *you* have a PSP, I mean have one of your own?" he asked Jo.

"Yes, here, have a go."

Mark took the PSP and explored it "I've seen these in adverts at the bus stop, but I've never had a go with one. Can you show me how to play?"

Jo and Mark settled down on a step near the window and Jo gave Mark a guided tour of the PSP. Ada looked back through the window at the glass blowing workshop and realised that a small women was beckoning to her and pointing to a door to her right. She pushed the door and went into the workshop. The woman greeted Ada.

"Hello. We're on the train but it's stopped at the station for a bit. I really need to stretch my legs!" Ada explained.

The woman, Greta, showed Ada around. "As you can see," she said "We use traditional glass blowing methods here and the colours are provided by the minerals found naturally."

Ada was struck by the lack of technology "How are your orders taken and the deliveries tracked?" she asked.

"We use a paper based system that has been in place for many years. George over there is our expert; he can explain more of the detail." Greta pointed to a man sitting at a desk near the far wall of the workshop.

"We are hoping to be able to buy a computer soon to record this information and eventually to advertise our products," she explained. "I know a little about computers because a bus comes along to my village twice a week to offer people the chance to learn about using a computer. However, there is not a reliable source of electricity at the workshop, so that means we need a backup power source as well as a computer, so it's not that straightforward."

"What about the Internet?" asked Ada

"Well, I know a little about that, but I don't get much chance to use it, because the nearest access point is twenty km away. We do hope to have it at workshop eventually, but that's not imminent."

"Have you thought about using a modem and a phone line to access the Internet? I noticed someone using a mobile phone on my way into the workshop so even if there is no landline, that might be an option."

"That might be possible," agreed Greta "but the costs might make this difficult and the phone network coverage is not that good." Ada started to appreciate that the situation was not straightforward.

"Do most of the workers here know how to use a computer?" she asked.

"They all know about computers to an extent. They know that businesses all over the world use computers and that it's important for us, and especially for our children, to learn how to use them. However, most of them do not actually know how to use a computer themselves," explained Greta.

"So would any of them have a computer at home?" asked Ada.

Greta looked a little surprised. "At home? No, nobody. I think that a couple of people are like me and go along to the bus when it visits their village. There is a computer at the library too and I have tried using that, but it's hard to remember what to do when you don't get to use it very often."

"Yes, I can see how hard that must make it," said Ada thoughtfully. Her eye was caught by a shelf of particularly bright and cheery glasses and she moved to take a closer look.

The train whistle sounded and Ada and Jo realised they needed to get back on board. The boys had enjoyed the PSP and Jo felt a little sad to be leaving. Mark might not have used a PSP before, but he was very quick to work out how to use it and turned out to be a worthy opponent for him. Better than Alex, at any rate.

Greta wished Ada a safe journey and Ada bought one of the turquoise glasses with silver and bronze beads. "It'll make a great present for my mother."

As they headed back to the carriage they bumped into Alex and Jerome who were looking a little breathless and pink. They had to run as they had wandered rather a long way from the station in a vain search for the famous Lippizzaner ponies.

They all climbed on board to find Chris asleep in the carriage. They tried not to wake her, but of course they did. She asked about the station and Alex, still a little breathless, replied "It was really small and we went for miles and miles and miles looking for ponies, but there were none anywhere, not one anywhere at all!" she stated with a large hand gesture.

Jerome decided not to correct the exaggerated distance in Alex's description and just added "I think it was probably a little cold for the ponies today, Alex."

"How about you two?" Chris enquired of Jo and Ada

"I had a great game of KnightCastle with Mark, this boy we met outside some glass making place. He had never used a PSP before."

"Hah," said Alex, I thought all boys had a PSP."

"Well not everyone has access to the same sorts or amounts of technology," explained Chris.

"Yes, this glass blowing place was out of the dark ages," added Jo, who had not been impressed "Nothing at all to do with technology in that place."

"Well, you say that Jo, but actually if it was not for craftsmen like the ones we saw who understand about glass and know how different types of glass can be made with different properties we wouldn't have things like the lovely touch screen on the myone, so perhaps there is a bit more technology there than you think."

Jo had to admit that he had not known about that and grudgingly admitted it was true that the glass was very colourful. Ada took out the present she bought for her mother to show the others and told them about her conversation with Greta.

"But I wonder if mobile phones might help them out pretty soon," she added.

Jo looked surprised. "Places like that won't get mobile phones," he said. "They're years behind."

"That's what you think," Ada responded. "You remember my friend Jess in Kenya?"

"Children with jiggers in their feet!" said Jo. "How could I forget? You're not telling me they all have mobile phones?"

"Not exactly," Ada said. "But Jess tells me that though there is no phone line—in fact no electricity lines either—anywhere near

The digital divide

the village she's in, there are a couple of mobile phones that people share."

"Well how do they charge them up then?" asked Chris

"Solar panels," said Ada. "There's a community hut which charges up a big battery from solar panels for lighting so people can come and read when it's dark."

"But how can two phones in a whole village be useful?" Jerome asked curiously.

"Shared ownership. Though there are only two handsets, maybe a dozen people have got sim cards and they switch the handsets around so all of them can make and receive calls and texts."

"That's interesting," said Chris "I'd assumed that the important thing was the access to the technology and that if people had it then that was enough. But this makes me think that it's important that they can see how to adapt the technology to meet their needs."

"Yes," agreed Jerome "People need to understand enough about what the technology can do to see how they can appropriate it for their own purposes."

As Ada talked about Greta and the problems people in more remote parts of the world face when it comes to using technology, Jo picked up the turquoise glass and started to feel its smoothness and to notice how the colours changed as they picked up different amounts of light.

"This feels really nice," he said "It's almost like a joystick too if I hold it upside down, I can just imagine having these beads as buttons and then being able to see the game through the glass rim here," he said. "*Wow*, that would be so cool!"

Ada was getting nervous about her mother's present. "Oi! Careful, Jo! Good idea, though!"

At the fair

"Are we there yet?" asked Alex for the fifteenth time.

"Yes!" replied everyone else in exasperation.

"Finally!" she said. She had been looking forward to getting out and seeing the fair for the last few hours. The train rolled into the station.

"How long will the train stop here?" asked Ada.

"Two hours," said Chris, "They have to get fresh supplies and I think they will hook up a few more carriages. Do you have your packed lunch?" Sometimes Chris tended to forget that Ada was not one of the children.

"I think I might stay here and do some work," she said.

Chris said "Are you sure you don't want to come? This is a celebration you know, of the town of Hilarion's five hundredth anniversary. That is what that fair is about—showing life in medieval times."

Ada wasn't particularly interested in medieval life, but it occurred to her that there might be an internet café with a faster broadband connection in the station.

"Oh OK," she said.

Chris gathered the children and Jerome and bundled them off the train. They kept a look out for the conductor in his bilious

At the fair

yellow uniform in case he had a regulation about how they should disembark. Luckily, he was half way down the platform, probably still looking for the boy who tried to climb in the window.

They stood blinking in the sunshine, pleased to be out of doors after being in the carriage for so long.

"I haven't got my land legs yet," laughed Jerome.

The sound of drums and flutes drifted towards them over the market square. Jo spotted two knights in full armour in horses getting ready for a jousting tournament. Everybody formed a big circle around them. Alex said "I can't see anything."

Jo lifted her up onto his shoulders so she could have a better view. They watched it for a little while and then Chris suggested that they move over towards the medieval tents.

"Look at all the pretty flags," said Alex.

They made their way through the crowds. Chris noticed a tent which had a sign advertising "Learning with stories."

"Let's go in here!" said Chris

"Boring!" said the children, predictably. "I want one of those big toffee apples," added Alex.

Jerome took pity on Chris who had been looking after the children for so long.

"Why don't I take Alex and Jo to get some food and we can meet you back here in half an hour?" he offered. He was getting quite fond of Alex and Jo, although he didn't normally spend much time with children outside his research work.

Chris nodded her thanks.

A Medieval Tale

"Please come in," the friendly looking woman invited. She was wearing a long woollen orange skirt with a red tight fighting corset and a white bonnet. Chris assumed this was a medieval costume, although perhaps it was the height of fashion in Hilarion.

"Thank you," said Chris. "I saw on the sign that you work with storytelling. I'd like to hear a bit more about that."

At that moment she spotted a familiar red-haired figure walking by outside.

"Excuse me for a moment," she said and went out the tent. "Hello Peter," she said.

"Oh hello," he said with evident pleasure.

"I'm just going to hear something about storytelling. Do you want to come too?"

"Sounds interesting," he said perhaps not entirely sincerely.

Back in the tent, the Hilarion teacher was opening her laptop. It looked strangely incongruous with her costume.

"Just a moment," she said.

Chris wondered if she had made mistake. She didn't realise computers were involved and couldn't really imagine what she would need a laptop for. She briefly considered doing what Alex would do: shouting 'Boring!' and running away.

"Excuse me," she said politely, "but I thought this was about storytelling."

Peter, on the hand, had brightened up. "Should we give this a try anyway?" he coaxed.

Once the other teacher had set up the laptop, she turned towards them and said "Let me introduce myself. My name's Hilda

A Medieval Tale

and I have been part of this project of developing a storytelling resource for children with disabilities."

Chris looked even more surprised. "If children have disabilities the last thing they need is a laptop," she thought.

Peter said "I'm Peter and this is Chris. We are both teachers too. We are on our way to the Future of Learning festival. I'm the IT specialist teacher for our school. I'm interested in your project because there are some children with special needs in our school and I'm always on the look-out for new software."

"This might interest you then," she said, indicating the software which was loading on her laptop.

"*A Medieval Tale*,[37]" read Chris. "I love the art work. It has a medieval look. How do you use it? Isn't it too difficult for the children?"

---

[37] Gjedde, L. (2006). Story-based e-learning as a vehicle for inclusive education. Current developments in technology-assisted education. A. Méndez-Vilas, Solano Martín, A., Mesa González, J.A., Mesa González, J. . Seville, FORMATEX. **2:** 1126-1130.

Inside Stories: A Narrative Journey

A screen shot from *A Medieval Tale*

"Oh no," said Hilda "My pupils love it. I have a pupil with various functional deficits. He has cerebral palsy and can't control his movements. He can't even speak. It has been really difficult finding software which was relevant for his age because most software packages which is meant for easy navigation has very childish content. It is not interesting for a teenager to work with software that is only two yellow ducks moving on a screen."

Peter nodded. He knew exactly the problem.

Hilda looked up as more visitors entered the tent. "Oh, here are some children now," said Hilda. "Would you like to play with this program?"

Chris recognised the messy face smeared in toffee. "Hello Alex" she said. "Back so soon?"

Jo said "Oh, can I have a go?"

A Medieval Tale

Jerome peered at the screen over his spectacles. Hilda noticed that this dapper man appeared to have a tattoo on his cheek. It looked like a fish of some kind. Maybe he was a sailor.

"Hello," he said genially. "I'm Jerome."

"Hello Jerome, I'm Hilda. I'm a teacher. And what do you do?"

"I'm a professor of education."

"How odd," thought Hilda.

Chris watched in fascination as Jo opened the menu page.

"Story mode, theme mode, video mode and activity mode," she read. "Let's have the story"

"Yeah!" said Alex crowding in for a better look.

Chris was quite enchanted by the animated tale that unfolded. She loved the narrator's voice and the soothing music.

"I find the children are calmed by the music. They can work with this program for hours on their own. I find it a wonderful ambience in the classroom," Hilda explained.

Chris thought how different that sounded compared to the noise and disturbance she had always felt radiating from the computer room at school.

"I've never seen software like this. This is like a film isn't it?" she said as the narrator told the story of Sir Gavin and Lady Ragnell and how Sir Gavin saved King Arthur's life by finding the answer to the riddle of what women desire the most.

"Not quite like a film. You can do activities," said Hilda as they reached the first side story in the software where the user could explore a stop in the knight's journey. Even before she said that, Jo had activated the dressing game. Alex snatched the mouse and started to drag new clothes onto the character on screen, dressing her up in medieval clothes.

"She looks like you now," she told Hilda.

Hilda answered "One of the things that means a lot to children with disabilities who cannot talk is that they can do these activities for themselves. For instance, they can dress themselves up because we put their photo on the character and then they can print out what they have done and take it home to show their families."

She pointed to a display behind the computer. They turned to look at it. There were several photos of children and teenagers, all beaming with pride. Some were in wheelchairs with medieval houses in the background.

Dressing up for the Medieval Tale project

Jerome said "Some of these children look like they are dressed up for real. That can't be done in a computer, can it?"

A Medieval Tale

Hilda said "Well we used the software to introduce the children to the medieval culture, stories, music, images. You see, everything in the software is based on authentic material. But of course we want the children to have real life experiences too. So once we had used the software for some weeks we arranged for a visit to a medieval life centre where the children could dress up for real. They could even cook medieval food and take part in colouring and weaving of cloth and watch a real blacksmith work."

"Cool!" said Alex.

Jo was now absorbed in a cooking game in the software. He laughed. "Look at the boot!" he said. On the screen there was a bubbling soup pot with ingredients arranged around the side so the children could make their own choices of what to cook. Jo had just dropped a boot into the pot.

A screenshot of *A Medieval Tale*: soup game

"Ooh! Do a mouse next!" shouted Alex, laughing.

Hilda said "This activity is a favourite with my class too."

Even Jerome got into the spirit of things. "Put in a hen!" he advised. The ingredients jumped out of the soup pot at irregular intervals, impossible to predict.

"Let's go on with the story" said Chris after a bit.

"Let me have the mouse now," Alex said.

Chris said to Jo "You should help Alex."

Jo looked scornful. "It's easy," he said. "She can do it herself."

Alex could indeed do it. She swiftly navigated until she was back in the story. They watched the story until it came to another activity.

"Look! Musicians!" she said. "I'm going to try this one."

There was a page with empty musical staves, with a line for a series of different medieval instruments. As Alex selected the flute they all heard a flute melody. Jo said "It's my turn," and selected a drum. The drum rhythm joined the flute.

"Oh," Chris said. "You're making music."

Peter said "This sounds like real medieval music on period instruments."

Hilda "I've been working with this activity for months in a class with students with severe disabilities. It was so exciting because they cannot speak and we did not know if they understood anything. But then they kept choosing the same instruments over and over again and when we were doing it in class they would get upset if somebody else chose their instrument. So they obviously understood far more than I would ever have thought. Now we have even given them the real instruments so they can hold them and try them out."

A Medieval Tale

Peter asked "What about the videos? I saw that was one of the modes."

Hilda told Jo to click on one of the figures. A video opened of a woman weaving. Peter watched for a while. "That certainly looks authentic," he said. "I can see how that could be used in history or arts subjects."

"Yes, it worked very well combining the videos with the real life experiences at the medieval centre. This was a way to revisit the experience and try to talk about it. The children also loved watching the videos for hours. This is good because there is so little they can do on their own."

"I want to know what happens in the story," said Alex, taking back the mouse and navigating back again.

Chris turned to Jerome "This is a frame story, isn't it?" she said. "Like I did with the sea project."

Jerome said "Yes, this a more tightly integrated frame story because all the activities are contained within one story."

Sir Gavin was posed a riddle.

"What do women want the most?" repeated Peter. "I wish I knew."

Jerome looked at him in sympathy. "Money?" he pondered.

"A good looking man?"

"Chocolate?" suggested Jo.

"Horses!" said Alex.

Hilda smiled. "Just wait and see," she said.

They watched to the end.

"No way!" said Jo when he heard the answer to the riddle[38].

---

[38] If you want to know the answer, look up Sir Gavin and Lady Ragnell in your local library. Or google them.

"Of course," said Chris approvingly.

"Errr...of course." Peter said glancing at Chris.

"I wouldn't have thought of that," said Jerome.

"Do you think Lady Ragnell got to keep Sir Gavin's horse?" Alex asked. "Can I make a story now?"

"Yes, you can," said Hilda. She showed Alex how to get started. Alex chose a female knight character, ignoring Jo's comments that there were no such things. Chris looked even more interested as Alex easily chose the other elements in the story, ending up liberating the prince. She was able to have the story read aloud when it was finished.

"Oh," she said. "This could be quite useful, I guess. Sometimes you need something really simple to get children going with their storytelling. I can see how this would work." She suddenly glanced at her watch. "Goodness!" she said. "We'll need to hurry to get back to the train."

"Plenty of time," said Peter.

"Thank you so much for all you've shown us. I've learned such a lot," Chris said to Hilda.

Hilda gave them each a leaflet and Jo took photo of everyone standing next to Hilda in her costume.

Jerome stayed to asked Hilda one last question. "What difference does it really make for challenged learners to use technology? I would think the laptop would be quite expensive, and it must have cost a lot to produce this program. Would you say it was worth it? I mean, there must be so many things that your learners need—so how did you come to choose this one?"

"As you know, severely challenged children have very little choice. They are so dependent on helpers all the time. This software is a way of giving them more choice. It's a way for my pupils to express more of the child that is caught within a body that is difficult to use."

"The story was about Lady Ragnell having a choice, wasn't it?" said Alex, who had come to drag Jerome away by the hand.

Jerome was impressed by the teacher's sincerity and her commitment to her class. Not to mention her flattering medieval attire.

"It's been a real privilege to meet you," he said. "The work you are doing is wonderful!"

Hilda blushed. "I do my best," she said. "Would you like a copy of the software?"

"I certainly would!" Jerome exclaimed but hoping that Ada could help him set it up.

Jerome as mermaid man

Chris had agreed to meet Peter for a drink, so she went to the restaurant car, glad to be away from Ada's technology for a while. She was getting more interested in technology after the conversations that afternoon and seeing the demonstration of *A Medieval Tale* in the morning. She still couldn't see herself juggling a classroom full of kids and computers at the same time but she had an uneasy feeling of something unavoidable to come. Peter's enthusiasm was infectious and she thought he might talk her into some kind of computer project. Still, it would be nice to have a rest from Jerome's theorising to try something out for real.

Peter greeted her "How's the journey so far?"

"OK," she sighed. "Like being trapped in a cage with two monkeys, a gibbon, and a wizened old orang-utan."

Peter laughed. "I know the feeling," he said. "My class are driving me nuts. But I think your kids are doing quite well. The lad seems very bright and interested."

"Jo?" asked Chris in surprise "Really? The other teachers were very pleased to have him out of the classroom to come on this trip. He gets stroppy quickly."

"Sometimes you see that with the boys. Give them a computer and they are transformed."

"Into little geeks," thought Chris. "A bit like you really," but she didn't say it aloud.

Peter went on, thinking what a good listener Chris was. "One of the reasons I decided to become an ICT specialist in the school was that I saw this happen to a boy I had totally given up on. He suddenly started to work and I must say I was surprised at the quality of what he produced on the computer. He never used to hand-in his homework and was the first out of the room when the bell rang. And then he started to sit in the play-times to finish his work. It was a miracle!"

Chris was surprised to hear him use that word. "A miracle?" she repeated.

"Yes," he went on. "He even started his own company while he was still at school. It was like a whole new world had opened for him. He turned out to be incredibly bright."

Chris was slightly suspicious. She had been a teacher for many years and she had yet to see a boy that she had given up on have such a spectacular success. But then she thought of one of her pupils who was really struggling. Maybe she owed it to him to find out more about computers in case it would help him.

"Tell me what I could do to get going with computers in my class," she said.

"Have you done any work on a computer yourself?"

"I use the computer as my typewriter. I need to use it to make materials and letters for the parents. I don't use email though because the local authority keep changing my email address and then I lost some messages."

"You could do a simple project to get started. Have you got a digital camera?"

"Yes."

"Then you could do a project with digital storytelling since you are so interested in that sort of thing."

"Can you show me?"

He had his digital camera in his laptop bag. "Typical," thought Chris. "Doesn't go anywhere without it," but she liked it that he wanted to help.

Peter said, "I have never tried using this to make a story, but I think we could use a presentation program like PowerPoint or Keynote, to make a little comic strip story [39]."

"Okay! The children love comics. But I don't know what we should have a story about. The comics are always about superheroes aren't they?"

---

[39] Or you could use a dedicated software package like *Comic Life* or *Kar2ouche*.

"Well, not quite," said Peter. "But we could have a story where a superhero rescues the train. They're always doing that." He was pleased to show off his own creative skills, but he wouldn't admit to knowing too much about comics. He didn't want to look like a geek, after all.

"What a geek," thought Chris, but she was quite surprised that he so easily came up with an idea for a story, since he had seen so uncertain on his own abilities in that area.

"Who's going to be the hero then?" said Peter modestly yet hopefully. Chris looked at him, "Nice smile, but too scrawny to be a hero," she thought.

"How about Jerome?" she said with a grin.

"What, that old guy we went to the fair with?"

"Yes," she paused, "No, he would never agree."

Peter said "He needn't know. I'll show you what we can do with a digital camera and some software. Go and get a photo of Jerome." He handed her the camera and pointed to the button, "Just press this, and the rest is automatic."

Chris grinned again and set off down the corridor.

Peter opened up his presentation program on the laptop and looked for other images which might be suitable.

"I got it," said Chris. "What do you want to with it?"

"I'll download it unto my laptop." He looked closely at the photo. "Does he have a mermaid on his cheek?" he said.

"Don't ask," said Chris.

"I wish it had been a dragon," said Peter, "It would fit a superhero better."

"He could be Mermaid Man," said Chris, who was getting a bit giggly.

Jerome as mermaid man

"Fantastic," said Peter, "Let's give him a tail."

He pushed a napkin towards Chris and said, "Draw me a mermaid's tail then."

Chris looked bewildered "But how...?"

"Just draw it," he said, "and I'll show you."

Chris sketched the tail and passed it back to Peter. He took a photo of it and downloaded it to the computer again.

"Now look," he said and opened the photos up in a photo-program.

"Which program is this?" she asked, wondering if her computer would have something like that.

"Oh, it doesn't matter," he said, "most cameras come with free software and most of them have the same kinds of tools. They are really simple to use, you just need to learn a few principles and then you are in business. I'll show you how to cut something from on picture and paste it into another," he said. "Most packages have got a lasso tool which you use for selecting."

He selected the mermaid's tail "Now I'm going to cut it," he said. "Most packages have a cut option on the edit menu. It is really this simple, just look!"

He switched to the picture of Jerome. "Now we have to decide exactly where to put it. Do you think this looks right?"

"Oh, let me try!" said Chris, laughing. "It suits him."

When she was happy with the position of Jerome tail Peter showed her how to paste it in place.

"Perfect," he said, "Mermaid Man is ready to rule the world."

"Who should he rescue?" said Chris

"How about the kids?" said Peter.

"I'm not sure they deserve to be rescued," said Chris.

"He could rescue the beautiful young teacher who is looking after them then."

Chris blushed and looked away. "Let's just make it the kids" she said.

They worked together for a while, then copied the pictures into the presentation program. Chris typed captions under the pictures and Peter showed her how to do speech bubbles.

"Do you want to record a narration too?" he asked.

"Oh, could we?" Chris said, "That would be great!"

Peter showed her how to turn on the audio recording program, and she spoke into the microphone built into the top of the laptop screen.

"Should we have a look at how it has turned out?" asked Peter.

He switched to slideshow mode in the program and Chris could see their cartoon strip full screen. The narration played in the background.

"*Wow*, that's *easy*," she said, "I thought it was much more difficult. I can see how I could maybe even make it work with my class. But maybe it would still be more difficult with all the children. And what if they get stuck? I can't be everywhere at once."

"Do you remember how you told me before that your children were peer-tutoring when you did your sea-life stories project? You said the kids were able to learn a lot from each other. Well it's similar with this kind of technology project. You'll find that there will be some kids in the class who already know a lot about computers or digital cameras, or videos, or whatever you're using. They love to be experts in something, so they are usually happy to help the other children. You can take the role of facilitating children who are working together, and giving the advice about the storyline and so on. I think it helps if you acknowledge from the start that there is no way you can know everything about the technology."

"You mean: admit it to the kids?" asked Chris.

"Yes! Of course, you learn the basic skills yourself to start with, but you can make it clear to the class from the start that everyone is learning together and that when someone learns something interesting they should share it with other people. I build it into plenary discussions with the kids. I get them to talk about the technical problems they had, and if they solved them and other people can offer advice. I suppose it's teaching problem solving.'"

"I hadn't thought of it like that."

"And resilience. You know we keep getting those memos round about how we're meant to be teaching the children to be successful learners? Well, these sorts of projects do that!"

Chris knew the memos he meant. "I've often wondered how you actually teach the skills they mention. Like 'determination to succeed' and so on. The skills all sound really great and you can't argue with them, but it never tells you how to develop them."

"I've certainly found that technology projects work for exactly these sorts of skills. Reasoned evaluation, creative thinking, working independently, all that stuff. I think it's partly because the technology is so motivating that the kids want to use it in the first place. Then they enjoy creating cartoons or films and they are so pleased when they see what they can produce that they keep trying even if it goes wrong. Because technology is never straightforward and full of tricky bits but yet you can do so much with it, it raises all these problems and hurdles. If you want to be optimistic, you can say these are just opportunities for developing successful learner skills."

"That's the kind of thing you would see in one of those motivational posters: every problem is an opportunity to learn something new!" Chris mocked gently.

"Yeah, the kind that would have a picture of a cute kitten on it or something. But you know what I mean. If you don't mind learning with the children, you can model the sorts of strategies to use when you need to solve a problem or find out something new. In the end, that's what the kids need to be able to do. They need to come across a problem in real life and figure out for themselves how to solve it."

"I wish I was as confident as you are about it all," she said.

"It takes a bit of practice at first, just to get familiar with it. I can help with that. And it's useful if there is another teacher at work who wants to learn with you. Then you can help each other out."

"Hello Chris! And Peter is it?" Jerome was picking his way towards them through the crowded restaurant car.

"Hide it! Hide it!" yelped Chris.

Peter shut the laptop lid.

"I'm just getting some exercise. I got tired of sitting in the carriage." Jerome said. He caught Peter's eye and noted vaguely that Chris looked a bit agitated. He continued quickly "I don't mean to intrude. I'm sure you're having a nice chat. Maybe I will join you later." He smiled at them both and wandered off.

"He's a decent bloke," said Peter.

"Oh dear. I was so embarrassed. What if he saw Mermaid Man? We should never have used his photo like that without asking."

"Well, I wouldn't let the kids do it in the class for sure. But I bet Jerome would be quite flattered really. Who doesn't want to be a super-hero?"

Fear of technology

"Did you have a nice chat with Peter?" asked Jerome when Chris came back into the carriage.

Chris looked flustered. "Errr. Yes, thank you. He was showing me how to do a comic book," she said, hoping that Jerome wouldn't question her further. "I am a bit worried about whether I would manage to do it with my class though."

"I'm sure you could," Jerome said, reassuringly, "Some years ago I was peripherally involved in a project to help young children develop simple multimedia stories—just imagine a cartoon strip with characters, scenes, speech bubbles and so on.[40] It sounds quite similar. In fact, the teacher in that project had never really liked computers and was very worried that she could not cope."

"Sounds like plenty of teachers I have met," said Chris, "Technology really freaks them out. Me too!"

---

[40] This section describes theT'riffic Tales project. Cooper, B. and P. Brna (2000). "Classroom conundrums: The use of a participant design methodology." <u>Educational Technology and Society</u> **3**(4): 85--100.

"The project was using some quite unusual equipment for back then," continued Jerome, "including the use of a large back projected touch sensitive screen and individual workstations also with touch sensitive small screens."

"My electronic whiteboard hasn't been installed yet," commented Chris.

"As it happened, she took to using this equipment very fast and before long was getting children to create stories together with her," Jerome declared "She was in the habit of getting her young children to sit down on a mat every day to listen to a story. She was a natural storyteller—the children would be wide eyed and enthusiastic and she would always get them to answer questions and come up to the blackboard and provide bits and pieces that helped the story along. And once the technology was installed, the class would sit on the same old mat and now she used her story telling skills to involve the children in building stories on the computer. She assimilated the new technology into her existing good practice."

"That's great," Chris said, "Did the children like the techie gear?"

"The children were wide eyed, keen to answer questions and very excited to be asked to come up to the big touch screen and add elements to the story," Jerome said. "They were always amazed when, with a single touch of their finger on the screen they could bring a wizard into the story—and they really enjoyed dragging characters around with their fingertips to place them somewhere new."

"Yes, the kids do love that. One of my friends from college uses electronic whiteboard all the time."

Fear of technology

Jerome thought for a while, and said "The teacher was so encouraging to children, sitting low beside the screen, she treated them almost as equals, never intimidating them. The children always loved her lessons."

Chris sighed. "Those lessons sound really good. It's quite frustrating that we have the hardware in our school but it hasn't been set up yet. Mind you, I am not sure I would have the confidence to try it," she paused. "Well I might, actually. I got on quite well with the programs Peter showed me, and I liked Hilda's software!"

"There always will be teachers who find it hard to cope with technology. But it sounds like you are learning very fast. A willingness to learn new things is a good start. My colleague told me that the really important factor in introducing story creation software into the classroom was that the teacher was already an effective teacher with clear ideas of what her children needed to do and learn."

"But how did they cope with technological disasters? You know, when you switch on the computer and it doesn't do anything you ask," asked Chris.

"You are right that is a problem," agreed Jerome "Provided the technology was robust enough, she could share the problem of managing unfamiliar software and hardware by working with the class."

"That's what Peter said too," said Chris.

"The class also had several workstations placed around an octagonal table so the children could talk to each other," said Jerome.

"Why?" asked Chris.

"They used to share their knowledge with each other of how to make the software do what they wanted and what to do in difficult situations when the hardware and software misbehaved."

"So the children were the key?"

"Yes," Jerome nodded. "The teacher would go around and help out. As she did so, she learned so much about the software—and even about the hardware. It's a rare case of a software and hardware package which was designed with learning and human interaction in mind. It's far too rare, in my view."

Theatre in education

Ada, who had been listening with one ear, was gearing up to argue with Jerome about the merits of educational software but she was distracted when the door to the compartment slid open. To the surprise of all within, a solid-looking woman with a bright red face and huge green hat covered with plastic flowers stood there. Her long dress was as red as her face and she had a green shawl.

"Hello m'dears," she said. Everyone stared.

A shout came from down the corridor of the train.

"Hey, what do you think you are doing? Come here!"

A tall, thin man with a bright green face and a red pixie hat appeared next to the woman. He was dressed in a green tunic and leggings with a red cloak.

Theatre in education

The two of them started to argue. It became clear that the green man thought he had the right to tell the red woman what to do because she was his wife. She disagreed.

The argument ended with the woman declaring that she was thirsty and needed a cup of coffee.

"Come on now Mr Green," she said. "Since I took that cleaning job you told me I couldn't do I'm a woman of means. Come back down the train with me and I'll get you a cup of coffee too."

Mr Green looked deflated. "I liked the good old days when the men did the buying," he said morosely. "How can I be a gentleman if you buy the coffee?"

The woman smiled. "The coffee tastes the same. Don't be a gentleman and I won't be a lady. Let's just be friends. Come on!"

She turned to go, but as she did she handed a small leaflet to Jerome, who was sitting nearest to the door. And she winked at him. Then she took the green man's arm and they went off together.

There is a moment of stunned silence after they left. Then Alex leapt over to Jerome.

"What's the leaflet? Who were they? Were they real?"

"The Green and Red Theatre in Education company," Jerome read off the leaflet.

"Did they seem real to you, Alex?"

Alex looked a bit taken aback by the question. "Well, sort of yes and sort of no," she said hesitantly.

"Of course they weren't real," said Jo in his best grown-up voice. "They were actors. But I thought they were pretty good," he added.

"I liked the woman," Alex said. "But that funny man was a real bossy boots. I don't think men should boss people about like that." She looked meaningfully at Jo. "Specially brothers."

"But I know more than you do," Jo said indignantly. "And I promised dad I'd look after you."

Everyone laughed, because this is so close to what Mr Green had said earlier when he had explained that men knew more than women and had to look after them.

"See the power of theatre!" Jerome said, still chuckling. "An ounce of dramatic experience can be worth a ton of telling people about things sometimes."

"And that was something you couldn't have done with technology," Chris said, looking at Ada. "Real people doing real interaction must be better than sitting in front of a computer or even using a myone."

"Theatre in Education is exceptionally good for areas where behaviour and attitudes rather than knowledge are important," said Jerome, in a more serious tone. "The key is creating strong, relevant, memorable experiences—and using theatrical technique to summon up imaginary but believable worlds."

This left a bit of a silence as everyone else tried to digest what he meant.

"I liked those actors," Jo said slowly. "But when we had some round at school last term, it didn't work so well."

"Why was that?" Chris asked, interested. "Were the actors no good?"

"No, it wasn't that at all," Jo said. "It was just that they weren't doing the same stuff as these actors. I thought they were kind of funny bickering like that. The ones we had were doing a play about bullying. It was all a bit heavy for me."

"Some of the big boys have been nasty to my brother," Alex said brightly. "Coz he has dys...dys..."

"Dyslexia," said Chris.

Jo scowled at Alex. "That's right, blabbermouth, tell the world."

"But Jo, if you don't tell anyone, how can anyone help?" Ada asked in a reasonable tone. "Some of the girls used to get on at me when I was at school because I was into what they called boys' stuff—computers, and technology. There was one nasty little piece of work called Daphne Stevens who saw herself as queen of the class, and she as always making snotty remarks. She'd tell me that nobody wanted to do group work with me, or people were meeting up at the weekend but I wasn't invited. It really got me down for a while."

"So did you tell someone?" asked Jo.

"I talked it over with my mum," Ada said. "She worked for a big computer company, so I guess it was down to her I got interested in technology. She convinced me that Daphne was being a bully and it wasn't that there was actually anything wrong with me. That made me feel a lot better."

"But didn't you tell your form teacher?" asked Chris, sounding a bit shocked.

"Mr Graham?" Ada said, surprised. "I didn't think he'd understand girls' stuff like that. Anyway, my mum suggested I look around for someone else who was into technology and do stuff with them, and I joined the computer club. I was better at computers than any of the boys that went, and then I met my best friend, Jane. She was in a different class and we didn't know we both liked technology. She stuck up for me and I stuck up for her and Daphne decided she wasn't getting anywhere and gave up."

"But surely a dramatisation of bullying is a really good way of raising the issue without any particular person having to tell a teacher," Jerome said. "Jo, didn't the school run workshops along with the play so people could talk about the problem together?"

"Well, yes," said Jo. "But you see I was in a workshop with Gaz and his mates and it's them that have been giving me a hard time. So I didn't feel like talking about it in front of everyone else did I?"

Simulation and drama

"I think that's something technology can help with then," said Ada to Jo. "Just let me download a piece of software I remember coming across and then you can have a go at it."

"Me too!" said Alex.

"Software?" asked Chris. "Surely that can't work anything like a theatre company? Knowing about bullying isn't the same thing as dealing with it at all."

"This is a virtual drama," said Ada. "It's called *FearNot!*[41] and it has graphical children in a graphical school. It is applying ideas

---

[41] See Hall, L., Woods, S. and Aylett, R. (2006). "FearNot! Involving children in the design of a Virtual Learning Environment." International Journal of AI in Education **16**(4): 327-351 and also www.e-circus.org

Simulation and drama

from live theatre I think—apparently you see a kid being bullied and then get asked to give him some advice which influences what he does the next time it happens. From what I've read it's aimed at kids a bit older than Alex and quite a bit younger than Jo, ten year olds. So Jo may find it a bit beneath him. Still, Jo, you get to play with it on your own, which means at least you can think about the problem without having nasty types like Gaz around. See what you think."

While she had been talking, the software had been downloading, and at this point she handed the laptop over to Jo.

"Here you are," she said briskly. "I think it has sound on it, so use your earplugs. Alex—you have a go after Jo, don't crowd him like that."

Alex moved away, looking cross and stared out of the window restlessly.

"Are you sure this is really a good idea?" Chris asked. "Isn't this some kind of a computer game? I hope it's not a 'zap the bully' sort of thing? That would really trivialise a very serious problem."

"Some games company has already done that one [42]," Ada said cynically. "Shock factors sell copies for some companies. Although, to be fair, there are also Serious Games [43]. Games technology can be used for education rather than just for entertainment. Not always as monotonous as shooting monsters."

---

[42] Rockstar. "Canis Canem Edit." Retrieved 29th May, 2008, from http://www.rockstargames.com/canis/home/.
[43] See Wikipedia, c. (19 May 2008 19:53 UTC). "Serious game." Retrieved 29 May 2008 16:20 UTC, from http://en.wikipedia.org/w/index.php?title=Serious_game&oldid=213537549.

Inside Stories: A Narrative Journey

"Of course," said Chris. "There are some very good games for teaching primary mathematics. I often use those. But anti-bullying education is not like learning about prime numbers."

"Serious Games often look at much more complex educational issues than arithmetic," Ada told her. "The Games for Change [44] group focuses on social issues and social change—there's one produced by the UN about distributing malaria nets for example; there is even one about the genocide that took place in Rwanda. You can't get much more serious than that."

Chris looked appalled. "How could I use software that showed a massacre? That might seriously upset the children."

"Worse if it didn't," said Ada, seriously. "It really happened after all."

"But I don't suppose it focuses on bloody corpses," said Jerome.

"No, I think you role-play a mother who has to soothe her crying baby to avoid the soldiers finding her."

"That way the player would identify with the terror of the victims without the need for blood and gore," said Jerome. "It would use empathy, as I assume the game that Jo is playing tries to do, and as a Theatre-in-Education production would too. Drama need not be a simulation of reality you know. Actors on a stage often cannot simulate reality anyway."

"People always think computer games are like simulation but they needn't be. I think it's because computer games look a bit like films," said Ada. "Films look very real even though you know they aren't, if you think about it."

---

[44]. "Games for Change." Retrieved 29th May, 2008, from http://www.gamesforchange.org/

Simulation and drama

"Let's ask Jo whether *FearNot!* is a simulation or drama," suggested Jerome.

Alex heard this and immediately jumped up from beside the window. "My turn!" she squawked. She pulled one of the earplugs out of Jo's ear and he jumped to swipe at her, luckily without making contact.

"Hey, get off, I was just getting into this."

"But it's my turn," Alex insisted.

"Jo, maybe you can tell us what *FearNot!* is like," Jerome suggested. "And Alex can have a go while you do."

"OK, I suppose," said Jo, still looking cross.

He handed the laptop pointedly to Ada rather than to Alex.

"Wait a sec," Ada told Alex. "I need to restart it—as far as I know there are different dramas for girls and boys."

"What did you think of it?" Chris asked Jo curiously.

"Well, you can see it's for younger kids," Jo said. "The kind of bullying that goes on in the school isn't as bad as it gets when you're older. And the characters look about 10 too. But it's weird, you do end up feeling quite sorry for John, and you want to help him."

"How life-like is it then?" Chris wanted to know.

"Oh, the characters are cartoony, and so is the school," Jo told her. "And you can tell how they feel because they get big grins or really obvious miserable mouths. It's not nearly as slick as stuff I have on my PSP. But the stories are pretty good all the same—the sort of stuff I remember from primary."

"And do you get to bash the bullies?" Ada asked, grinning.

"Oh no," Jo said. "You don't get to be in the scenes at all, you just have to watch and hope John took some notice of what you told him. But it makes you think."

Violence in games

After a bit Chris moved to sit next to Alex and watched the screen of Ada's laptop with interest. Alex was watching a story unfold.

A screen shot from FearNot! (1)

"That's not fair" thought Alex. "I really feel sorry for John. Just because he works hard!"

A screen shot from FearNot! (2)

Violence in games

Alex weighed up the situation. "I know the teacher wouldn't like it but maybe John should hit Luke. Then he might stop."

A screen shot from FearNot! (3)

"Right!" thought Alex. "I *will* tell John to punch him. That'll show him."

Chris screwed up her face when she saw Alex type this advice.

A screen shot from FearNot! (4)

"I wonder if John will do what I told him?" thought Alex. "Maybe he'll be too scared to hit Luke though."

"I'm not at all sure this software is a good idea," Chris remarked to Ada. "Alex is telling the character who is being bullied to punch the child who is victimising him. That's not good advice at all. And now one of the characters has pushed the other one over. I think this will just encourage children to behave badly."

"But how can you get kids to think about bullying without showing some of the things that happen?" asked Ada. "Anyway, when I was having all that trouble at school my mum told me that if anyone hit me, I should hit them back only harder. Never happened though because Daphne Stevens wasn't into actual violence, just nasty remarks. She'd have loved it if I'd lost my cool and lashed out at her and I wasn't quite stupid enough ever to do that."

"Well I told John to hit Luke back too," said Jo. "I know teachers don't like it but it does work sometimes. Though actually when John tried it, it made Luke cross and he pushed John back a lot harder, so I guess it wasn't such good advice after all."

"There you are," said Ada. "The software isn't teaching people to be violent at all. Sounds more as if it's showing the downside of violence."

"There's been a great deal of research into violence in computer games," Jerome told them. "To some extent you could say it's a moral panic—once it was comics that were thought to be teaching children bad behaviour. 'Penny dreadfuls' they were called. After that it was children's cartoons or the Saturday morning films, and then television. Even the lyrics of a type of popular music—'rap' I think it's called—have been blamed for causing violent behaviour."

"But it can't be good for children to see characters being violent to each other," Chris said. "I can see that this anti-bullying software doesn't let the child actually be violent themselves, but what about video games where the whole point is to shoot people?"

"But it's fun shooting things in games," protested Jo. "It's not like it make you want to do it for real. I can tell the difference you know—I'm not *that* stupid! When I've had a bad day at school and I'm feeling screwed up it makes me feel a lot better to blast a few game characters."

"There is some evidence that adolescents who play a lot of violent video games are more aggressive in real life[45]," Jerome commented.

"But that doesn't prove the games *make* people like that," Ada said. "Could be that more aggressive people like playing more aggressive games."

"That's a very good point," said Jerome. "In fact the biggest review of all the studies carried out so far[46] found that no causal link had been established. It also pointed out that many of the experiments were badly organised and not at all like the way people used games in real life."

"If you think about it," says Ada, "a lot of fairy stories have violence in them. What about the giant in Jack and the Beanstalk? 'I'll grind your bones to make my bread'. Doesn't sound much of a pacifist to me."

"But fairy stories don't take place in the real world," Chris argued. "It's not like one child pushing another in a virtual school. That's what the anti-bullying software shows."

"Yes, but John did better when I suggested he find a friend to help him," said Jo. "I remembered what Ada said."

Ada smiled. Then she turned to Alex, still using the software on her laptop. "Even so, I think I'd like my laptop back now. I've

---

[45] Anderson, C. (2003, 29th May 2008). "Violent Video Games: Myths, Facts, and Unanswered Questions." Psychological science agenda Retrieved 5, 15, from http://www.apa.org/science/psa/sb-anderson.html.
[46] Freedman, J. L. (2002). Media violence and its effect on aggression : assessing the scientific evidence. Toronto ; London, University of Toronto Press.

got stuff to prepare for the conference. Oi, monkey! Unplug!" She tapped Alex on the arm and when Alex looked up, she removed her earplugs.

The advantages of unpredictability

Alex looked cross. "I'd just begun to really help John," she said. "And I'm not a monkey."

"Could have fooled me. You don't want me to get to the conference and find my demos don't work, do you?" Ada chided. "You can use the software again later, but right now I've got work to do."

"Oh alright," said Alex glumly and handed the laptop over.

"So how did you get on, Sis?" Jo asked her.

Alex glared at him. She hated being called 'Sis' and Jo knew that.

"Bet I did better than you, fish-face. I liked it when John pushed Luke back though," Alex said. "Served Luke right!"

"But I thought Jo said that then Luke pushed John even harder?" Chris said.

"Yes" Jo said, at the same time as Alex said "No."

"Hey, it looks as if the software did different stuff for you than it did for me," Jo said, sounding interested.

"Well, the first time I told John to tell his teacher," Alex remembered. "And then Luke said the teacher had been on at him but it didn't stop him carrying on bullying John."

The advantages of unpredictability

Chris looked cross.

"I never bothered with that," Jo said. "Grassing to a teacher would just make things worse for John."

"Jo!" Chris said, shocked. "You should always tell your teacher if someone is bullying you."

Jo went a bit pink. He clearly didn't agree but didn't want to say so. Jerome came to his rescue.

"The standard advice is to tell *someone*," he said. "It doesn't have to be a teacher if the victim doesn't want to. The really important thing with bullying is not to suffer in silence. You could tell someone outside of school for example, like a parent. Or someone your own age, like a friend."

"I did talk to dad about it," Jo said. "But he thought I had to fight my own battles and it would toughen me up a bit. He thought giving Gaz a punch would be a good bet, but like I saw in the software, that could be a really bad move. Gaz goes round with a gang and they're not short of muscle. I think Ada's mum had a better idea. So after hitting back didn't work I told John to try and find a friend to help him. He told a character called Paul about being bullied. Paul helped stand up to Luke with him."

"Oh," said Alex. "Paul was in a scene after I told John to punch Luke and he asked if anything was wrong but John said he was OK. Maybe I should have said 'tell a friend' and then he might have told Paul about it."

"Don't you think it's interesting how these different outcomes are provoking discussion?" Jerome asked Chris.

"I'm still not sure about this software," Chris said, "but I can see that if it adapts to different answers from different children that would be good for discussion. Maybe it could be useful after all."

"It's a bit like having your own theatre company, just for you" Jo said.

Massively multiplayer online games

"Do you play *World of Warcraft*, Ada?" Jo asked.

"Sure I do," said Ada.

"Cool," said Jo enviously. "My friend has it, but my mum won't pay the subscription. Are you Horde or Alliance?"

"Alliance. I have a level 60 Night Elf and a few other characters I keep around."

"What are you talking about?" asked Jerome. He was beginning to realise that there might be interesting new concepts embedded in Ada's geek talk, if only he could figure out what she meant.

"*World of Warcraft*? *WoW*? It's an MMO. Like *Lineage* and *Everquest*. Or *StarWars Galaxies*."

Jerome shook his head, pencil poised ready the take notes.

"OK," said Ada patiently. "MMO stands for massively multiplayer online game. They started out from text based online games like MUDS. MUDS are Multi User Dungeons. Maybe you played them in the '80s? They're sometimes based on dungeon and dragon rule-sets. The idea is that you explore a fictional world which is described in text. You might start off with a description of a room typed on the screen. Like: 'You are in a long dark hallway. Far away you hear a clanking sound. There are stairs up and doors to the north and south.' And then the player would type 'go north' and then he would get another description. He might collect objects to use later or meet characters who would give him riddles."

"I remember that! I used to play a game called *Granny's Garden*[47] when I was in primary school." said Chris unexpectedly. "You had to solve riddles to rescue children from a witch."

"I know the one you mean," said Ada. "The difference between that and what I was describing is the number of players involved. Massively multiplayer games really are massive. It's not like *Unreal Tournament* or other shooter games where you might play with tens of other people a time. *World of Warcraft* has over 10 million subscribers[48]. That's more than the population of New York City! Isn't that crazy?"

She typed on her laptop for a moment. "Hang on, let's see. I'll just find the stats for *Second Life*[49]. Right. 13 million residents. Over a million logins in the last 60 days. You often find that people will sign in to these things a couple of time to look around and then lose interest. So the number of active players, or residents as they are called in *Second Life*, is smaller than the headline figures."

"But that's still a huge number of people," said Chris. "More than the population of the town where I live. More pupils than I will teach in a life time."

---

[47] 4Nation. "Retro Granny's Garden." Retrieved 29th May, 2008, from http://www.4mation.co.uk/retro/retrogranny.html.
[48] Blizzard Entertainment. "World of Warcraft reaches new milestone: 10 million subscribers." Retrieved 29th May, 2008, from http://www.blizzard.com/us/press/080122.html.
[49] Linden Research. "Economic Statistics." Retrieved 29th May, 2008, from http://secondlife.com/whatis/economy_stats.php.

"I would think so," grinned Ada "Unless we discover the cure for ageing sometime soon. It's a huge technical challenge to keep these worlds online. All those players doing so many different things, making changes which affect each other and the world around them. You can't expect the game world to be the same next time you log on. The other players may have done something to change it."

"What is the attraction for these players?" asked Jerome. "Why do so many people play?"

"It's a good question," said Ada. "And worth taking the time to answer properly. There's a guy called Nick Yee at Stanford who did a three year study of players' motivations in MMOs. 30 000 participants, Jerome." [50]

Jerome rose to the challenge. "Such numbers might seem impressive, Ada, but you know as well as I do that it is meaningless if the questions are not chosen carefully."

"Of course, I agree. Here, have the article if you want to check the methodology," said Ada waving her USB drive at him. "But my point is that his understanding of what motivates MMO players is based on a lot of data, rather than the sort of understanding a newspaper reporter might have after watching his next door neighbour play *WoW* for an hour. Ok, Chris, who do you think would play MMOs?"

"Ummm...," said Chris, suspecting a trap. "Teenage boys, I would think"

---

[50] Yee, N. (2006). "The Demographics, Motivations, and Derived Experiences of Users of Massively Multi-User Online Graphical Environments." Presence: Teleoperators & Virtual Environments 15(3): 309-329.

Massively multiplayer online games

"Nope!" said Ada. "The average age was 26, and the ages ranged between 11 and 68. It is 85% male, though."

"I would have thought so," said Chris. "I can't imagine women spending much time on games."

Ada was not going to let this past. "In fact, that's a myth too. If you look at the figures the Entertainment Software Association publish each year, 38% of gamers are female[51] Anyway, according to Yee's figures, 50% of MMO players have fulltime jobs, 36% are married and 22% have kids. And," she said, running her finger down a column of figures "13% of female players are homemakers."

"You mean, if I was playing *World of Warcraft*, I might be playing against someone's mum?" said Jo in disgust.

"Yes," said Ada "and I bet she would kick your ass"

Alex giggled. Chris raised her eyebrows at Ada.

"How long do the players spend playing?" asked Jerome.

"Twenty two hours a week on average," said Ada, checking the figure in the article.

"*Twenty two?*" choked Jerome.

"A *week?*" said Chris incredulously.

"That's what it says," said Ada. "Although bear in mind that there will be a selection bias in the survey. Maybe only people who are really into games chose to do a survey about it"

"That's like a part-time job," said Chris.

"Now I'm even more intrigued," said Jerome. "You still haven't told us why people are so motivated by such games"

---

[51] The Entertainment Software Association. "Essential Facts about the computer and video game industry 2007." Retrieved 29th May, 2008, from http://www.theesa.com/facts/pdfs/ESA_EF_2007.pdf.

Inside Stories: A Narrative Journey

"Imagine wasting all that time killing things that aren't really there," scoffed Chris in disproval.

"Hang on," said Ada, as she checked another file[52]. "It isn't that simple. In MMOs there are loads of things to do. You can go on quests, or learn new skills and crafts, go exploring, or role-play, or hang around chatting to people. Some people play MMO games without ever fighting. Anyway, Yee did a statistical factor analysis of his survey results and he found three main groupings of motivations: *achievement, socialising* and *immersion.* Achievement is probably closest to the common stereotype about why people play games. It includes advancing in the game to get to higher levels or win more points, and competing with other people but it also includes people who enjoy getting to grips with the underlying rules."

"Real dorks, then," said Jo.

"And immersion is about exploring the game world, finding new things and role playing characters. And escaping from real life."

"Escaping from real life 22 hours a week can't be healthy," said Chris.

"Maybe not" said Ada. "What would you rather people did?"

"I don't know. Go out in the fresh air? Meet their friends? Spend time with their families?"

"That brings us to the socialising category then," said Ada. "That involves talking to other people, making friends, relating to others and working in teams. Team work is a huge part of MMOs

---

[52] Yee, N. (2006). "Motivations for Play in Online Games." CyberPsychology & Behavior **9**(6): 772-775.

and you really need to understand that to understand what it's all about. When you think about this you need to get past the stereotype most people have in their heads of a spotty teenager alone in his bedroom playing space invaders. This is quite different."

"Hey!" said Jo, indignantly.

Chris was beginning to think that Ada, in her own way, was as bad as Jerome.

"What kind of team work do you mean?" asked Jerome. He was taking copious notes as was habitual to him when he first encountered a new topic of interest.

"Once you get past a certain level in *WoW* then some of the challenges are based on team efforts. It gets quite complex because there's a huge amount of strategy involved. Usually there's a guild leader or someone who takes responsibility for coordinating it all. Everyone has a different role. And after a campaign like that then everyone gets together to dissect it and discuss what went wrong and how they could fix it next time. Some people might go off and do some research to find out how they could improve the strategy. They have endless discussions about it on the forums. But the groups can be fluid; you don't always work with the same people. It depends who's in the game at the time."

"Those sound like quite useful skills," acknowledged Chris, "The lecturers at college used to always go on about transferable skills that employers like: team work, leadership and so on."

"Yeah," said Ada. "There's this guy called John Seely Brown who wrote an article for *Wired*[53] about how employers were

---

[53] Seely Brown, J. a. T., J. (2006). You Play World of Warcraft? You're Hired! <u>Wired</u>.

recruiting people who wrote they were guild leaders on their CVs. A bit weird, if you ask me. Over hyped."

"Very interesting," said Jerome. "Group learning, but motivated by interest. Self managed learning, Communities of practice?"

"In fact," said Ada, glancing surreptitiously at the file open in front of her, "you could say that there are 'complex forms of socially and materially distributed cognition, including coordination of people, (virtual) tools, artefacts and text, across multiple multimedia, multimodal "attentional spaces."'" [54]

"Come again?" said Chris somewhat resentfully.

Jerome stopped writing and stared at Ada. "Fascinating," he said. "Are you by any chance quoting someone?"

Ada laughed "Course! You didn't think I would use a turn of phrase like that did you? It's from a paper by a friend of mine. She did her PhD using virtual ethnography with *Everquest*."

"What's that?" asked Jo.

"It means she hung around in *Everquest* for nine months or so taking part and talking to people. And keeping lots of notes to study how everyone worked with each other."

"No way! Was it like her job? I want to do that when I grow up!" said Jo, envious.

"It also mentions something called reciprocal apprenticeships where one player teaches another a specific skill which they in turn might have learnt from someone else. It's got an example

---

[54] Ada is quoting from p12 of Steinkuehler, C. (2008). "Massively Multiplayer Online Games as an Educational Technology: And Outline for Research." Educational Technology 48(1): 10-21.

where one player gives scaffolding to another to help her learn a new skill. You're into all that stuff, aren't you Jerome?"

"Indeed, I have a passing familiarity with the works of Vygotsky," agreed Jerome with gentle irony.

"Hey, Chris, you'll like this," said Ada, looking at the file again. "It's talking about teenage kids who spend 2-3 months working in their spare time writing stories about the game world. I mean it's not part of the game itself, but it's tied into it. So they like to write stories to expand on their characters or back story." She laughed "There's an example of a kid who wrote a story and posted it for his online friends to read—but he admitted he really wrote it to hit on a girl he liked!"

Chris snorted. "Chatting up girls with stories? That'll be the day!"

Jo shuddered. "Sick!"

"What about stories, though?" asked Chris. "Does the game itself have a storyline?"

Ada thought. "Mmm. Not exactly. I suppose you could say the stories are emergent: the story lines are different depending on what the player or group of players gets up to in any given session. It's as if the game designers put in ingredients for a story—the basic bones of a quest, or maybe come up with new features for special events like Valentine's Day. After that it's up to the players themselves to make of it what they will.".

"The players improvise?" asked Jerome.

"Like in story drama?" asked Chris. "I do that sometimes in the class where I set up a scenario and the kids take different roles and a story sort of falls out of what they improvise. Sometimes I lead the direction of the story, but usually in the role of a story character."

"In a way," said Ada. "But the game designers set it all up in advance and don't take part as characters. I mean they couldn't be playing 24 hours a day to keep the story going. They do respond to what the players seem to want by building new features. They keep a close eye on things."

"That sounds fun," said Chris. "It must be really hard to design ingredients which might turn into an interesting story in advance"

"There's a huge art to it," said Ada. "And it really depends on the players' imaginations too. It helps the designers out when the players just love these games and really throw themselves into it."

"I wonder if I could do something like that with my class?" mused Chris.

"Do you mean make a virtual world with story ingredients in it?" asked Ada.

"Yes," said Chris cautiously, hoping that Ada wasn't going to make her do it right there and then.

"I'll help," said Alex, looking up from her fairy tales book. "I'm good at making games now," she said with supreme confidence.

"That would be great," said Ada. "I would have loved to do that at school. I don't think I would use *WoW* though. It's got too many weird game rules built in so it would be quite hard for your kids to get the hang of. You could try *Second Life Teen Grid* or *Club Penguin*, though. I think the BBC are working on something similar.[55]"

---

[55] Conlan, T. (2007). BBC launches 'Second Life for kids'. Guardian. Manchester, Guardian News and Media Limited

"What is *Second Life* exactly?" said Jerome.

"It's a 3D world which is built entirely by the users. Unlike *WoW*, where the world is mostly built by game developers. Linden Labs, the company behind it, provided a set of tools so people could sculpt their own world. You can visit it for free, and also buy your own land. My university has a private island. It's dead easy to make your own objects and clothes and things once you are in the world. There's a programming language too so you can make your objects do anything you want. At the moment people are trying out what could be done with it in education. There's a whole lot of speculation about how fabulous and 21st century-esque it would be to teach classes in *Second Life*. It's mostly for education, but there's a project called Schome[56] where the researchers explored using *Second Life Teen Grid* with a group of kids to learn philosophy and physics for example"

"How would I use it for stories, though?"

"If you wanted something for your class, you could buy an island on the teen grid and make your own story ingredients—a castle, or a haunted house, or a marshy swamp—and then let the kids loose to improvise. They could make characters and communicate with each other either by typing or voice chat."

"I suppose it would be useful for them to practice their writing by typing the lines their characters would say," said Chris. "It wouldn't be so daunting to them to have to write in little bits."

"Way back in the mists of time (starting in 1998 or something) there was a researcher who did work on that," said Ada. "It was a

---

[56] Schome. (2008). "The education system for the information age." Retrieved 29th May, 2008, from http://www.schome.ac.uk/.

virtual drama system called *Ghostwriter*[57]. She looked at the stories children wrote after they improvised in role in a virtual environment. She compared them to the stories they wrote after a normal writing preparation activity in class and found that the drama environment helped the kids to write stories which contained more characterisation and dialogue. The kids loved it, and they discussed some interesting ethical issues which the story scenario brought up." She paused "I wonder what ever happened to her? She must be ancient by now."

"Going back to the story ingredients idea, is it is possible for the users to make their own content, could the children themselves not make the story world together?" asked Jerome. "In the same way as Jo and Alex made the game together?"

"I didn't think of that" said Ada. "Yes, you could do! You could teach them a bit of simple programming or do that bit for them. That reminds me... " she reached for her laptop again and started searching.

Chris noticed that it was second nature for Ada to use the laptop throughout her conversation. The keyboard was almost an extension of her wrist. "It's like travelling with a character in a sci-fi movie," she thought.

After a moment Ada said "You know what you might like, Alex? Lego have a new multiplayer online game called *Lego Universe*, due to be released in 2009.[58]"

"I love Lego!" said Alex.

---

[57] Robertson, J. and. Good., J. (2003). "Using a Collaborative Virtual Role-Play Environment to Foster Characterisation in Stories." Journal of Interactive Learning Research **14**(1): 4-29.
[58] Cavalli, E. (2008). "LEGO Universe: 'LEGO Star Wars Multiplied By A Million'." Retrieved 29th May, 2008, from http://blog.wired.com/games/2008/02/lego-universe-1.html.

"Lego rocks!" said Jo.

"Have a look at this then," said Ada, turning her laptop screen round so they could see a movie playing.[59] "It's a trailer for the game."

The children watched the colourful animated Lego men wandering around in a Lego city full of movement and activity.

"And the best bit is—you can build your own place made out of virtual Lego bricks online. And *then* you can order it as a real plastic Lego set to play with on your bedroom floor!"

"Oh *wow*," said Alex, overcome.

"Marvellous," said Jerome. "Think of the possibilities for transferring play between the real and virtual worlds. Between the imagined and the tangible."

"My class would just *love* that," said Chris. "It's such a nice idea. Think of the story worlds they could build that way."

She turned to Alex. "Why don't we draw what our Lego world would look like?"

"Pass me a pen," said Ada, "I want to do one too!"

The wonderful world of blogging

"What are you writing about, Ada?" asked Chris. She had noticed that Ada had been typing furiously for the last half hour, with even more intense concentration than normal.

---

[59] Crecente, B. "The Lego Universe Trailer." Retrieved 29th May, 2008, from http://kotaku.com/gaming/exclusive/the-lego-universe-trailer-271566.php.

"Oh, just blogging," said Ada, "Catching up with the trip so far. Friends at home wanted to know how the trip is going so I thought I should update them"

"Blogging?" asked Chris. "I think I read about that, but I don't really remember…"

"Come on, Chris!" said Ada, impatiently, "Do you not use computers at all?"

"We can't all be as geeky as you are," said Peter, coming to Chris's rescue.

"I'm the first to admit I'm a card-carrying geek," said Ada, pointing at her t-shirt which said 'Free the mallocs'. Chris looked at it, none the wiser. "But it's not just geeks who blog. The whole point of Web 2.0 and social networking is that it's user driven, not developer driven."

Chris caught Peter's eye in a mute plea.

"Shut up for a moment, Ada," said Peter. "Chris, "blog" is short for weblog. It's often used as an online diary, but sometimes it can be a collection of news items or pictures which someone collates together for other people to look at. Ada's is a diary. You can make blogs private so only you and your friends can look at them, or you can have them open for everyone in the world to see. A really useful feature is that readers can leave comments for authors to read. You can get whole conversations with lots of different people on comments pages."

"Oh," said Chris doubtfully "But why would people want to read other people's blogs?" She was really wondering why people would read Ada's blog. Maybe other geeks would, but ordinary people?

The wonderful world of blogging

"Sometimes because they're well written, or funny, or because they are about a topic you are interested in, or because they give you information you need. Really it's about communication. You can set it up so that every time someone posts a new entry to their blog you get the update. You can always stay in touch."

"I think the Guardian online does something like that," said Chris. "Sometimes readers leave comments on news stories."

"Exactly," said Peter. "And as you can imagine, it has huge potential in education."

"I *can't* imagine," said Chris dryly. "Convince me."

"Do you remember at college the lecturers used to tell us how it was important to give the pupils a sense of audience when they're writing?"

"Yes," said Chris, on safer ground "Kids find it hard to imagine what a reader needs to know so they leave out important details. Or else they write with the teacher in mind, with the teachers' background knowledge, and so it doesn't make sense for a general reader."

"You see!" said Peter "Blogs give kids a real audience. My class have a blog. Actually, all the classes in my school have them. We had a chap from Learning and Teaching Scotland come to our LEA and do a talk on why blogging was good in education. Ewan McIntosh[60], his name was. He had a huge blog audience himself. He managed to convince people they should be blogging too, so we started this year. It's been great fun. Here—Ada, lend me your laptop for a moment."

---

[60] McIntosh, E. "Social participative media, education and the future." Retrieved 29th May, 2008, from http://edu.blogs.com/edublogs/.

Ada sighed and saved her blog post. "Alright," she said, handing it over.

Peter typed an address into a web browser. "Look Chris," he said "This is our blog for the class. It's all about an animation project we've just finished."

Chris tilted the screen so she could see it more clearly. "Oh yes!" she said "You've got pictures of the characters the children used."

"And videos," said Peter, pressing a button. Jo peered over the top of the laptop. "That's cool!" he said. "Can I see?" He squeezed into the seat next to Chris so he could see better.

Chris laughed as the animation came to a close with a flourish. "They recorded their own voice-overs too," she noted. "That's really nice."

"I wanted to show you the writing though," said Peter. "In this section I asked everyone to write about the storyline for their animation. And then they left comments for each other for peer review."

"Their writing is good," said Chris, reading with a practiced eye. "You must have worked hard with them."

Peter beamed at her.

"I wonder…" thought Ada, looking from one to the other.

"Is that a comment from a parent?" continued Chris.

Peter looked where she pointed. "Yes, I was really pleased that the parents showed an interest in the project. Some of them like to catch up on what the kids are doing in class. You know what it's like when kids come home from school and their mum asks them what they did at school. They usually say 'nothing' so it's good to convince the parents we actually do work occasionally."

The wonderful world of blogging

Chris laughed. "I can see your point. Still, I do good peer writing and reviewing with my class just with pen and paper and it works pretty well."

"Of course. Blogging is a convenient way to reach more people, though. But look at this," Peter clicked on another page. "We got a nice surprise one day because we got a comment from a teacher in Australia. Her class had been looking at for animations on the web, and they found ours. The kids were delighted that other children so far away were taking an interest, so we kept posting our animations for each other to see. My kids liked blogging so much they would nag me if I forgot about the blog for a day. 'We have to blog about this' they kept saying."

"Imagine kids clamouring to do functional writing," remarked Chris. "Although of course they could have ordinary pen friends."

Ada butted in "The point of blogging is that it's a genuine audience. Little communities of people form around a shared interest. Here both classes were interested in animation at the same time so it made sense for them to communicate. But they might link up with another class—or several classes—if they have a different project in common. With ordinary pen friends you can't really know if your friends will have shared interests to start with and the process is so slow that you lose the immediacy."

"There's a bit in your magazine about it," said Jo who had been flicking through Ada's *New Scientist*[61] earlier. He found the page. "It says 83 blogs are created every minute of the day," he read from a headline. "And this graph says there are 112.8 million blogs being tracked by Technocrati. What's that Ada?"

---

[61] Gillmor, D. (2008). Bloggers and mash. New Scientist. London, UK, Reed Business Information Ltd. **197:** 44-47.

Inside Stories: A Narrative Journey

"Technocrati is like Google for blogs," said Ada.

"112 million? That's a lot of authors," admitted Chris. "And how many readers?"

Ada pointed at another chart. "Look, 45% of US consumers create their own content for others to see. Like blogs or websites or videos. And 69% of consumers view content created by others. So there are more people viewing than making, as you'd expect. You get lots of hype around it, of course. All this talk of citizen journalism, and Web 2.0 and user generated content. But it is pretty radical. The news and entertainment isn't totally controlled only by media companies any more. Ordinary people can have their message heard."

"User generated content?" queried Chris.

"You know, blogs and wikis and podcasts and YouTube videos. Stuff which people make themselves and stick online for other people to see."

"My class did podcasts when we were learning about World War 2," said Peter. "They did mini radio shows. It was loads of fun."

Ada took back her laptop. "Chris, let's have a look for stuff on storytelling. I bet there is loads out there." She hunted for a moment and then said "Yeah, I thought there would be. Look, this is a blog from a storyteller,[62]" she handed the laptop to Chris.

"Oh how lovely!" said Chris. "She's got lots of articles and suggestions, and look she's even got audio recordings of her stories!"

---

[62] Hedman, R. (2008). "Storyteller's Social Networking: Top Three Sites." Retrieved 29th May, 2008, from http://storytellingadventures.blogspot.com/2008/02/storytellers-social-networking-one-site.html.

The wonderful world of blogging

"I bet she's not as good as telling stories as you," said Peter.

"Yip," Ada thought. "He's smitten."

Chris read through the web site for a while, plainly pleased to have found a like-minded soul online. After a while, she asked "It has an article on storytelling networks. It mentions Linked-In and Facebook. What are they?"

"Social networking sites," said Peter. "You can use them to keep in touch with friends and colleagues and find out what they're doing. You should sign up to Facebook, Chris. We could stay in contact after the conference."

Ada smirked. Chris murmured something polite but non-committal.

"I thought Facebook was just for teenagers," said Chris. "But look, I searched for storytelling and there are lots and lots of groups for it—over 500. And events—hundreds of storytelling events all over the world."

"That's not that surprising," said Ada. "It's a natural fit, I would have thought."

"How do you mean?" asked Chris.

"It seems to me that you storytellers are a gregarious bunch," said Ada "You're always either telling stories or talking about them. I can just imagine when you get together you talk non-stop!"

Chris laughed. "Of course," she said.

"So of course it makes sense for storytellers to want to meet even more storytellers online; more people to natter and share ideas with. Putting audio recordings of your stories for everyone to hear is just another way for your stories to travel around. It seems like loads of the stories you tell are about other countries and cultures. Social networking would help put you in touch with people who are immersed in different cultures."

"Yes," said Chris thoughtfully. "I didn't see it that way before."

"Actually," said Ada, who could be quite persuasive if she put her mind to it "The parallels between storytelling and these technologies run deep. Both are about sharing and expressing your ideas, about reaching an audience. They're based on ordinary people's passion for communication. They're about hearing everyone's voice. In fact, there's a phrase which you often see in articles about Web 2.0 which fits: 'architecture of participation.' It's a technical term, of course, but don't you think that's exactly what a good storyteller provides? They provide the framework, perhaps the beginning of a story. And then the architecture extends upwards and outwards as the audience members participate, add to the story and maybe tell their own stories in response. All over the web, there are stories growing and extending and reaching new people."

Chris looked at Ada with renewed respect. "How well you put it," she said.

"Damn Ada," thought Peter enviously. "I wish I'd said that"

The future of narrative learning

Jerome's dream

Jerome stirred in his sleep. All the chocolate biscuits Alex had fed him sat uneasily in his stomach. He dreamed he was in a vaulted room with a high glass ceiling. There was a woman in a silver dress with lots of pockets standing next to him. She looked familiar in some way, particularly the blond spiky hair.

The air in the vault grew darker, and a faint green mist started to billow from the edges of the room, swirling closer and closer to where Jerome was sitting. The woman snapped her fingers rapidly three times and from the mist emerged a beast so fearsome that Jerome grew pale. It was a laptop with teeth longer and sharper than any other he had seen. The laptop advanced on him, snapping its jaws. The woman snapped her fingers three more times and the air was filled with the menacing chime of emails arriving. As the sound of the last chime died away, there came a quiet rustling sound, gradually getting louder as the emails came closer. The emails fluttered around and around Jerome, some of them settling on his body until he was neck deep in unanswered messages. He could do nothing but watch in horror as shuffling figures lurched clumsily into the hall. "Brains…" said the zombie students. "Lecture notes…", "Will this be in the exam?" The zombie students had their hands stretched out towards keyboards and their lifeless fingers never ceased typing. Jerome was horrified. He struggled but could not free himself from the mire of mail.

"Jerome," said Chris. "Wake up!" He mumbled and turned away from her, deep in his dream.

Inside Stories: A Narrative Journey

Jerome's Dream

Above the shrill sound of the mobile phones ringing, he heard a new, kinder, sound. It was the sound of mighty wings beating above the glass building. He looked up to see the silhouette of a winged horse against the darkness of the winter sky. With a mighty crash, Pegasus smashed through the class atrium and he was able to see

Jerome's dream

the rider. A mermaid was seated side saddle on the horse's back with the end of her tail gently extending over his broad back. The horse alighted next to him and reared onto his hind legs, kicking the front legs in the air. The neigh of Pegasus was so beautiful that it broke the spell of the sorceress and the sea of emails started to subside. The mobile phones were silenced and the laptops settled on the floors, lids closed.

He opened his eyes. Chris and Alex were looking at him curiously.

"You were dead to the world," said Chris.

"What were you dreaming about?" asked Alex. "You said 'Pegasus'. I heard you."

"I had a dream," said Jerome, dazed. "It was horrible. There were laptops snapping their jaws at me. And emails. The emails were burying me…" he trailed off, realising that Ada was looking at him in amusement.

"Jerome," said Alex solemnly. "Do you remember how you told me to make friends with the snake in my dream? You told me to talk to it."

Ada snorted with laughter. She held up her laptop, holding it at the hinges so she could flap the lid open and shut. She moved it across the table to Jerome. "Grrr," she said, "I am a ferocious laptop! See my flapping jaws! Face me, Jerome. I'm your friend really."

Alex giggled and stroked the laptop lid. "See Jerome, it's a friendly laptop."

Jerome loses his bag

Jerome tweaked Alex's nose, and got up to stretch. He decided he had better have another look at his keynote conference presentation to prepare for the next day.

"What *have* I done with it?" he muttered. He scratched his head and once more checked the luggage rack overhead.

"What are you missing, Jerome?" asked Ada.

"My briefcase. It has all my papers in it. Including my talk for the conference!" he said, anguished.

"Oh no!" said Ada sympathetically. "Was your laptop insured?"

"My laptop? Oh no, it's at home on my desk."

"Well do you still have your memory stick?" she asked. "CD, then," she added as Jerome shook his head hopelessly. "Surely you emailed it to someone?"

"No," said Jerome, sadly. "I wrote my paper out long hand with my favourite fountain pen and I was going to read it out."

"You're kidding!" said Ada in patent disbelief.

Jerome ignored this, and put his head in his hands. "I'm doing a keynote and it's tomorrow evening. How am I ever going to redo it in time?"

"Don't worry, Jerome," said Chris, patting him on the shoulder. "We'll all help. Won't we, Ada? I'm sure you could help Jerome on your computer."

"I'll draw a picture for you," said Alex, "And look, you can have my last Rolo if you like" she offered, handing him a squashed chocolate. She felt she should stand by him in his hour of need.

"No problem," said Ada "Just tell me what you want to say and I can help you make the slides. We can do an all-nighter if we need to. Jo, go get us all a can of coke."

Jerome acknowledged the good wishes and confectionary of his friends gratefully. He and Ada settled down next to each other and she opened the laptop.

"I wonder…" he said thoughtfully. "I think I may have changed what I need to say."

"How come?"

"The topic I was asked to talk about was 'The Future of Learning Technology'. I can only assume they asked me to talk about that so they would have some controversy."

"Controversial how?" asked Ada.

"Well I am fairly well known in the field for criticising the thoughtless use of technology in learning, whether it's for higher education or primary or secondary. I have expressed my views that the use of technology in education might be much over-rated. I think the organisers were hoping I might say that there was no future for technology in learning. Or perhaps that there was no future for learning if technology is involved. Something of that nature anyway."

"Hmmph," snorted Ada. "If you're going to say that, you're on your own, pal! You can sculpt your own slides on tablets of stone."

Jerome smiled at that. "My point, young Ada, is that I have now changed my mind about technology in learning from my discussions with you and Peter. And I have learned a lot from you, Jo. And you, Alex."

"We showed you how to make games, didn't we?" Alex said proudly.

"You did indeed. What I was going to say is that technology is not liberating us from mundane routine. Often it drags us down into even more pointless administration. Can you honestly say that email is a useful tool? Does it really make your working life easier? Or does it ensnare you in a cycle of pointless reading and typing about matters of little importance?"

"You might have a point there," conceded Ada.

"I have been involved in various university committees which study e-learning and how it could be used in higher education. But they always got bogged down in the very worst kind of dull record keeping. It was about recording and monitoring students, not about education! Education should be an organic, fluid process. It should be about people, not procedures. E-learning seemed to me to be the equivalent of having a filing cabinet on the internet where students could get copies of lectures. On this committee there was little recognition that learning at its best is not a transmission of knowledge from experts to novices, as in the instructivist tradition. It is a dialogue, a conversation between learners and experts, encouraging expression and reflection. And so the committee believed it was supporting distance learning by putting all materials on the internet, but gave no thought at all to what the experience of a distance learning student might be. There was no imagination. No innovation in teaching. I was ashamed to be part of it. So I resigned. A sad affair, very sad."

Chris looked at Ada apprehensively but she was nodding in agreement.

"You're right," she said. "You're right. But you shouldn't blame the technology itself. It's just a tool. A pen is a tool, and a whiteboard. Or even a text book. People need to know how to use the tools in sensible ways. It seems to me the problem you are talking about comes from the university trying to use new technology to do the same old thing they have always done. But it can be so much more if the committee had thought how the technology could solve some of the old problems in education instead of replicating them in a new medium. For example, take *Second Life*. Here you've got this great potential of a MMO and then people go and waste it. Every time I see a lecture theatre in *Second Life* it makes me wince. Why do universities go to all the trouble of making virtual versions of their own campus and then have students come to lectures in-world? I mean, you can easily and cheaply bore people in real life. So why would you want to recreate the boredom in a virtual space?"

"Quite," said Jerome, who had furtively checked his notebook to see what 'MMO' meant. "These massively multiplayer online games seem as if they could have great potential for communication and collaboration from what you said before. Again, resorting to the instructivist tradition (and the lecture format) seems to be the default behaviour for universities."

"I think schools are doing better than universities then, in this respect at least," said Chris. "A lot of teachers who have blogs with their classes. Then the parents can read about what the children are learning and comment on it. We're always trying to get parents involved in school life, and this technology is a way to do that. It lets us do something which is hard normally, as parents often can't make it to school during the school day but at least they can catch up in the evening. I really want to try it when I go back to school. I wanted to before but I didn't know how. Peter says he'll show me."

"I'll bet he will," thought Ada.

"Hmmm," mused Jerome, doodling on his open notebook. "Opening up the classroom to the real world. Letting the sunlight flood in."

"And letting the children's learning bounce out," laughed Chris.

"Are you going to put a story in your talk?" asked Alex.

"A story? No... I didn't intend to," said Jerome.

"Why not?" she said. "You're always talking about them."

"Although I have often studied the connection between stories and learning," he replied "I suppose I have not previously considered the connection between stories and technology. What might the connection be? Could you give me some examples?"

"What about the story we made in the game about the ghosts and the poison bottle?" asked Jo.

Jerome nodded and took out his notebook.

"And the lady we met at the fair who had the story about Sir Gawain in the computer program?" prompted Alex.

"Yes, I remember her."

"Or how about making comic strip stories?" said Chris "That can be loads of fun if you..." she tailed off as she remembered that Jerome hadn't been *directly* involved in that enterprise.

"You liked the *FearNot!* Demo I downloaded," Ada pointed out.

"Why don't you get screen shots of all of them and make them into a collage? That would look better than lots of writing," Jo suggested. "I'll show you how if you want."

"Of course, of course," Jerome was making notes now. "I think my talk may be rather different now. Yes indeed. But really I don't think there is time to pull all of these things together. It takes such a long time to prepare a key note. I would like to present this tomorrow, but there is no way I can put these new ideas into a coherent talk in a few hours. "

"Of course you can," said Ada, who was used to preparing things at the last moment.

"Of course you can," said Chris who had great faith in Jerome.

"How can I make sense of all these new things you have told me?" said Jerome distractedly.

Chris said "How do you normally organise your thinking?"

Jerome said "I prefer to make a diagram. That tends to strain out my thinking."

"OK," said Chris briskly. "Let's make a diagram then. Alex, lend us your pens." She could cope with helping people to make diagrams. She did it all the time in class. She unrolled a large sheet of paper which she had in her conference bag and taped it to the carriage window. "Jo, why don't you go and borrow Peter's laptop and make a collage of pictures of the software? Ada, start on the slides. And Alex, why don't you start drawing some pictures to decorate Jerome's slides?

"OK Jerome, let's have a go at it then. What do you consider the most important message you want to say?"

Jerome looked slightly embarrassed by her teacher's voice. It was a long while since anyone had addressed him in that particular tone. "Errrrr. Well. My original talk had a diagrammatic model of narrative learning." He stood up, trying to keep his balance while the train moved over a rough section of track. He sketched it on the large sheet of paper.

"Look, there's a spectrum with two end points: internal comprehension and meaning making and then external expression and construction. When the learner listens to stories, there is a dual process in which the learner hears the story and relates it to herself and her world. And then if she retells the story, there is an external process of expression and construction which will enable another listener to go through a similar cycle."

"What about when you imagine a new story?" asked Chris.

"That should typically have an idea or a theme and then you have an internal construction of the story around that. Of course then you normally tell the story to someone else, and so it moves into external expression at that point."

Chris doodled on the paper. She drew a couple of hearts, and as she coloured them in, she asked "I understand that" she said, "But it doesn't mention anything about the way people feel."

Jerome clung to the overhead luggage rack, nearly losing his balance as the train moved in uneven jerks. As the train lurched, he hit his head.

"What do you mean?" he said, sitting down, rubbing his head. "Aha! You're talking about the affective dimension!"

"Am I?" said Chris.

"Yes, yes!" Jerome jumped up again and grabbed a pen. "Previously I was focussing on cognition. But tell me more about what you mean. As a teacher, do you have any experiences about this?"

"It's so important to listen to the children and their stories and how they really feel about things. If you leave out the feelings and do not engage them in finding subjects and things that are relevant to them, then the feeling is left out. That's when they get bored and jump around like little monkeys!"

"I see," Jerome said. "So do you think that you can separate their thinking from their feeling?"

Luckily for Chris, she did not fully understand the theoretical consequences of such a question. She drew a coiled line swirling

Jerome loses his bag

from one side of Jerome's line to another. "I see it like this," she said. "On this side, you have feelings, and on this side you have thinking. But the learning goes back and forth between thinking and feeling all the time."

"It sounds like you are dividing feeling and thinking?" queried Jerome.

Chris answered "Well of course they are linked together. For practical reasons when planning my teaching I prefer to think of them as two different but related areas of learning."

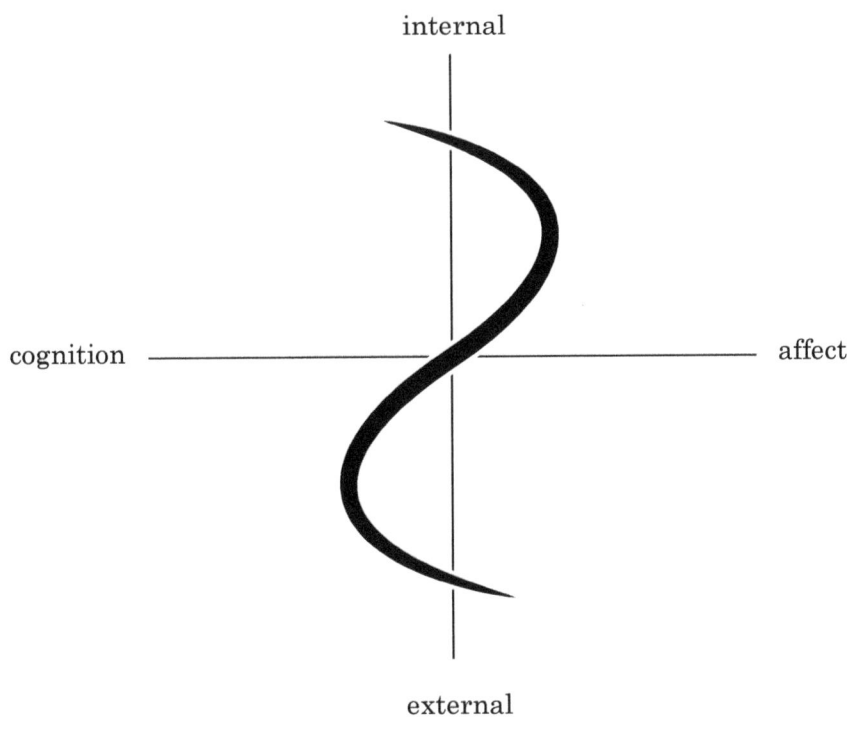

Jerome's diagram

Jerome started drawing again. "You mean like this?" he said dividing the drawing into four parts. "Do you think this would be a helpful model for you as a teacher to understand how to use narrative for learning?"

Chris lighted up in a smile. "How very nice to be asked by a researcher if things are usable! Yes, Jerome, I could make good use of your model when planning my story lessons."

Ada looked at the diagram. "I'll put that into your slides for you." She looked at it more closely. "Hey—Jerome! You've forgotten the technology. Again."

"What's that about technology?" asked Peter, sliding into the spare seat next to Chris and winking at her.

Jerome adopted his lecturer stance beside the diagram stuck on the window. "Obviously technology must have a place in this learning environment. But where?"

Peter looked amused. He knew this was a chance to impress Chris. "What about Papert's work on technology as a tool to think with [63]? You've got that bit on your diagram called 'cognition', so you could put in a label saying that technology can be a tool to think with."

Jerome pondered. "Papert? Oh that young American fellow?"

Peter raised his eyebrows. "Not so young, I would have thought."

Ada stood up to see better. "OK, if in the top left quarter here we are thinking of technology as a tool to think with, how about the box underneath? You labelled it 'external cognition'. What kind of tool do you reckon technology would be here?"

---

[63] Papert, S. (1980). <u>Mindstorms : children, computers and powerful ideas</u>. Brighton, Harvester.

Jerome loses his bag

"External cognition is about using external representations to grasp and construct meanings, perhaps in the form of a new story." said Jerome.

"Well that's obvious then," said Ada. "Technology is a tool to imagine with."

"*Imagine* with?" asked Peter. "How did you work that out?"

Ada looked impatient. "If you're using technology to make something new, like a digital comic or a digital animation or a game, then it's helping you to create something you couldn't ever do with pen and paper. It's a new medium for you to imagine in."

Peter said "Also, sometimes the kids find they get inspired by images or other things in software and it gives them new story ideas. Then the fact that there's an image to hold on to helps you to make a story."

Chris circled the bottom right of the diagram. "What about here, then?" she said. "External affect."

"I was thinking of expressing feelings by sharing and making new stories with other people when I wrote that," explained Jerome.

"That's a driving force in new media. You know, Web 2.0, and social networking and all that stuff," said Ada.

"Yeah," said Peter. "You remember I was telling you about blogs, Chris?"

Jerome looked back in his notebook. "I remember now," he said. "It takes me a moment to recollect what all this jargon means."

"You're one to talk," said Ada mildly.

"How about labelling it 'tools to share with'?" suggested Peter.

"Right," said Jerome, making further notes. "What about the last quadrant? Internal affect. This is where learners are making meaning from a story through empathising and identifying with characters. But surely this is where the tools analogy breaks down? How could technology be a tool to feel with?"

"Hmm," said Peter. "No, that doesn't work then."

Ada disagreed. "Well maybe not with the software you use in class about the moment. But there is some research software which I can think of which might fit the bill. How about *Fear Not!*?"

"I do see your point," said Jerome. "But what you are describing then, is not technology to feel *with*, but rather technology to feel *through*. In the same way as we discussed educational drama where the learner may experience emotional situations at a distance, a user of a well designed narrative learning environment may feel through the perspective of their avatar or on screen characters."

Chris looked dubious. "I still don't think you need computers to do that," she said.

Peter, loath as he was to disagree with Chris, said "But have you never been in the position in your class when you had to give up a project because you just didn't have time to spend with every individual kid? With programs like the one you described, or others like *Bubble Dialogues*[64] or *Working Things Out*[65], the kids can still be learning through feeling even if you aren't able to spend time on it directly."

---

[64] DialogBox. "Bubble Dialogue." Retrieved 29th May, 2008, from http://www.dialogbox.org.uk/intro.htm.
[65] ParentsPlus. "Working Things Out DVD." Retrieved 29th May, 2008, from http://www.parentsplus.ie/catproduct.php?pid=7.

Chris tutted. "An experienced teacher can always find time to include the needs of the individual child"

"Not all the time they can't," said Peter. "It would be great if they could, I agree. But look, Chris, we could argue all day about this but no amount of theory would convince you. You really need to try it out with your class to see for yourself. And then if it works, everyone has won. And if you don't like it, fair enough—everyone has a different way of working."

Jo had been thinking about what Chris said. "I don't want to talk about my feelings with my teacher," he said. "Urggh. It's really embarrassing. I would prefer to just work with the computer. Then it's private to me."

Jerome said "I understand what you mean, Jo."

"Well, I think the diagram is looking quite good now," said Chris. "Ada and Peter, why don't you go and make a neat version on the computer?"

"Yes ma'am," said Ada, but she took the drawing off the window anyway and opened her laptop again.

"Come on," said Chris to Jerome. "You look like you need some peace and quiet and a nice cup of tea to calm down"

Jerome allowed himself to be lead away to the restaurant car.

"That was really very helpful," Jerome said, adding some sugar to his tea. "Thank you. I'm pleased that I can integrate some of the things I can learned while travelling with you and the children into my talk."

"Yes," Chris said. She paused. "It's funny though. Because the talk is all about storytelling and learning, but there isn't a story in it. Just that diagram we drew."

Jerome nodded. "Alex did suggest I put a story in. But it is unusual. I mean, I have been giving talks for four decades and I have yet to tell a story."

"Well, you did say you had learned a lot of new things," said Chris. "Why not change the way you tell people about your ideas as well? I think the audience would like it." She wondered if she could persuade him. She charitably wanted to save the audience some of Jerome's worst excesses of theory, as she had suffered from it herself.

"Why not?" said Jerome with a sigh. "What story would I tell?"

"You could make a new one," said Chris tentatively.

Jerome put his head in his hands. "I can't," he groaned. "It's tomorrow." He wished this woman would go away and leave him in peace.

Chris gently touched his shoulder. "I'll help you," she said. "Why don't you just start from the beginning? It could begin like this 'There was an old man travelling in the bitter cold. He carried with him a sack in which all the knowledge he had collected from a long life was stored.'"

Jerome looked up. "Knowledge? I like that beginning."

"Go on," she said. "You can fill in the rest."

Journey end

Chris looked around the carriage. "How can five people possibly make such a mess?" she wondered.

Journey end

"Very easily," said Ada, "if one of them is Alex"

"That's not fair," said Alex. "Look at that pile of coke cans in your corner. Your teeth must be rotten"

Ada didn't bother to answer.

"Do you any of you know how to get to the hotel from the station?" Jerome asked.

Chris pulled the conference pack from her bag, but Ada had already taken myone from her capacious pocket. "Yip" she said. "I have it right here. We can follow the route with my GPS."

"Let's walk then," said Chris. "We need to some exercise."

"Do we have to?" groaned Jo.

"I'm so looking forward to sleeping in a proper bed tonight," said Ada longingly. "Those train bunks get pretty lumpy after a couple of nights."

Alex, Ada and Jo left the carriage, but Chris caught Jerome's elbow. "Wait!" she said, taking a tissue out of her pocket.

"What is it?" asked Jerome, watching in horror as she spat on the tissue and advanced towards him wielding it.

"You have a mark on your face," said Chris, hoping that Alex's marker pens weren't permanent. "Stay still!" she said, grabbing his arm and starting to scrub Alex's mermaid drawing.

"I can't think how I got a mark there," said Jerome. He hoped that none of his academic colleagues would pass the window and witness the sight of the teacher washing his face.

Wikipedia

The next morning, refreshed after a good night's sleep and some proper food, the travellers met again to visit the exhibition together. The highlight of the day would of course be Jerome's opening keynote talk in the evening, but some stands in the exhibition were already open. Chris had a little work to do on arranging her class exhibit for the next day so she turned Alex and Jo loose with strict instructions to report back in an hour. Ada was already touring the exhibition hall on the lookout for new gadgets.

Jerome surveyed the vast exhibition hall. There was so much to see—how could one possibly fit it all in? He decided to wander around and look for information on new technologies which he could include in his speech. Thanks to Ada and Peter, he was happy with his beautiful new slides and diagram. He was not so sure about his story yet. He had a glimmer of an idea, but he was stuck. "An old man walked through the snow," he rehearsed to himself. "He carried with him a sack in which all the knowledge he had collected from a long life was stored… But then what?"

He stopped to look at an exhibit which caught his eye. "*Wikipedia*—unleash your knowledge." He was all in favour of knowledge being unleashed. But what was *Wikipedia*? He recalled that Jo had mentioned it early on in the journey. The man standing at the display saw his interest and stepped forward to intercept him.

"Hello. My name's Jimmy. Are you interested in *Wikipedia*?" he asked.

"Pleased to meet you. I'm Jerome. I don't know much about it, but perhaps you enlighten me."

Wikipedia

"*Wikipedia* is an online encyclopaedia," explained Jimmy. "Do you know what a wiki is, first of all?"

Jerome looked at his shoes.

"It's OK," said Jimmy. "A wiki is collective online resource in which material can be added, edited and updated by a user community. The information in *Wikipedia* comes from readers of *Wikipedia*—effectively anyone who uses the web can add information to it."

This struck a chord with Jerome. "How interesting! The idea that the information is created by the readers is intriguing. But how would it work in practice?"

Jimmy nodded. "That's always the question, isn't it? Most people's first reaction is that it couldn't possibly work. They suggest that people wouldn't contribute, or else they would vandalise it, or that the information would be misleading. But this turns out not to be the case. Look, I'll show you." He lead Jerome onto his stand and pointed at the web browser on his laptop.

"My goodness," said Jerome, peering over the top of his glasses. "Over 2 million articles in English. And look at all these other languages too. Remarkable!"

"About 1500 articles are added a day, and there are about 45000 registered users[66]. It's the 37th most visited web site. You may have noticed this yourself—often now when you Google for something *Wikipedia* is the top hit."

Jerome decided not to admit that he wasn't in the habit of Googling for anything. "Just think of all those people contributing their knowledge to other people," he mused. "Wonderful."

---

[66] Giles, J. (2005). "Special report: Internet encyclopaedias go head to head." <u>Nature</u> **428**: 900-901.

Inside Stories: A Narrative Journey

"You might be interested in this," said Jimmy, spotting a fellow knowledge junkie. "Have a look at this visualisation[67]" He changed the web page, and Jerome saw a map of the world. For a moment nothing happened, then a bubble popped up over a map pin.

"Someone has edited an article about "Indonesian Idol" 3 minutes ago from the United States," Jimmy explained. "It doesn't show all the edits, just anonymous ones."

Jerome watched in fascination as map pins popped up all over the globe in a steady stream. "Imagine those people sitting at their computers all over the globe, contributing a little piece of knowledge to the world."

"They might not be sitting at their computers," pointed out Jimmy. "They might be using their phone or their PDA. Sitting on a beach somewhere."

"Obviously people do contribute," said Jerome. "But you raised a question about vandalism. Do you find people deliberately do that?"

"Yes, of course, but it isn't such a problem as you might initially think. A very interesting effect is that the user community curates the knowledge itself. Often someone else will quickly spot vandalism and correct it. Just as users can edit pages rapidly, edits can be undone rapidly. Users can also report vandalism to the administrator, and in very controversial pages, editing can be locked down completely for periods. People also track the quality of articles, and you often see pages which are marked are requiring further references or tidying up."

---

[67] Kozma, L. (2008). "WikipediaVision (beta)." Retrieved 29th May, 2008, from WikipediaVision (beta).

"I suppose that is important," said Jerome. "People need to recognise how reliable the knowledge they are reading is likely to be."

"Exactly," said Jimmy. "Shall we try out a topic so you can see for yourself? Give me a subject."

"Try folklore," suggested Jerome, thinking it might be useful to show Chris. He started reading the article. "Well, yes, fair enough. Mmm. Hmmph. Well, I wouldn't have put it quite like *that*."

Jimmy pointed at the top of the article "It says it needs citations for verification anyway," he said. "Why don't you fix it?"

"Me?" asked Jerome, surprised "I couldn't possibly..."

"If you don't, who will?" asked Jimmy. "All this knowledge is shared by everyone. If you don't think it's right, then don't you have a duty to fix it?"

Jerome stared at him. "I suppose I do," he said at last. "I suppose I do."

Jimmy showed Jerome how to edit *Wikipedia* pages, and left him to get on with it. He returned twenty minutes later with a cup of coffee each.

"How are you getting on?" he asked.

"It could be a lifetime's work making all those little changes," said Jerome. "But it is surprisingly comprehensive considering it is written organically. And the updates are so much faster than a print reference resource could ever be. Has anyone ever studied how accurate it is in general?"

"*Nature* did a small study in 2005," said Jimmy, pointing at a poster on the exhibition wall. "They got scientists to review 42 topics in their fields, and judge them for accuracy. It turned out that average number of inaccuracies in *Wikipedia* was four per article."

"Oh dear," said Jerome.

"But hang on!" said Jimmy "They compared it to Britannica. How many inaccuracies per article do you think they found there?"

"I don't know... none?" said Jerome. "I mean, they must check their facts."

"Three inaccuracies per article," said Jimmy, grinning. "So you see, the gold standard classroom reference resource isn't as golden as you might think."

"Apparently not," said Jerome. "Although you are right that people perceive it to be correct."

"This is the argument we're trying to make with this exhibition," explained Jimmy. "That we should be teaching children to be critical of information they read and question the sources of their knowledge. And not just on the Internet, but in print media also. It's the key to media literacy."

"Very laudable," said Jerome approvingly.

He thanked Jimmy and strolled out into the gardens where he had agreed to meet Chris. She was sitting on the grass making a daisy chain to give to Alex.

"Hello Jerome. What have you been up to?" she greeted him.

"I've been editing *Wikipedia*," he replied airily.

"Really?" said Chris in surprise. "Did Ada make you?" she added sympathetically.

Jerome laughed. "Not this time. But it turned out to be very interesting. Are you familiar with it?"

Wikipedia

"Peter showed me. He said his lecturer made the class edit *Wikipedia* articles at university to practice scientific writing. It made me think. It's a little bit like stories in a way."

"What do you mean?"

"Do you remember we talked about how there are different versions of the same story in different cultures? And how stories change and evolve as they pass from teller to teller? Each storyteller changes the story, or adds to it and then passes it on. That's similar to what happens on *Wikipedia* in a way. Except you can see how the article has changed if you want to with *Wikipedia*, and you can't really trace how a story has evolved when you listen to it."

"Very true," said Jerome. "That's a good point, Chris. I wonder if there is a similar resource for collecting stories." He passed her several daisies with long stems that he had gathered for her.

"I believe there are," said Chris, adding the daisies to her chain. "Several. Peter told me that *wiki* refers to the type of technology where the community edits the knowledge, and that *Wikipedia* is only one example. He said I could set up my own story wiki, but that sounds a bit complicated"

Jerome agreed and then said "There is another parallel with storytelling here. I noticed when I was watching the map which showed the *Wikipedia* updates that people were often writing articles about something local to them, for example about their town or school. Articles on such so-called minor topics would never make it into an official encyclopaedia. But it is important for the people involved—they could share something which was important to them directly with people who wanted to know. And for many years, stories have been a way for people to share their culture and personal experience directly with others. Except with this kind of technology, you can reach out to many people who you would never normally have a chance to meet face to face."

"Meeting face to face is important," argued Chris, threading another daisy into the chain. "You can't do everything with technology."

"Indeed not!" said Jerome. "I am the first to agree with that. But it seems to me now that there is a place for technology to extend, rather than replace, what we already do."

"Maybe," sighed Chris. "Come on, let's go and give Alex her daisy chain."

Physical interfaces

"Oh, excellent!" said Jo. "Come and see this, Jerome. I bet I can beat you at boxing."

"Boxing?"

Jerome looked at the stand. There were crowds of people gathered round watching as children played games together. Although they were watching large flat panel displays, they weren't sitting still at a keyboard. The players were jumping, throwing, strumming and even dancing as they used the technology.

"Look," said Jo. "They're playing Wii sports. And they've got a dance mat and *Guitar Hero* as well."

Physical interfaces

They watched together for a while. The Wii was a games console[68] which connected to the television. The unusual thing about it as far as Jerome could see, was that the players used a device like a remote control to play. As they waved the remote control (the *wiimote*, as Jo corrected Jerome), their character on screen would make the same movement. At first they were too far back in the crowd to see much, but when the loud speaker announced that the next session was due to start Jerome and Jo found themselves alone on the stand.

"Alright, Jerome, big man! Let's rumble," said Jo, with the smallest touch of irony. He handed him the wiimote and a second controller. "That's the nunchuck. Let's play *Wii Sports*. We'll do the boxing one. Hold the controllers up in front of you like boxing gloves. That's it."

The physical education teacher who was exhibiting on the stand came over to watch. He suppressed a smile at the sight of the dapper gent holding the controllers with such concentration.

"Your character is the one on the left. If you punch, he punches. See?"

"Gracious," said Jerome. "I see!" He tried another few experimental punches.

"Now!" said Jo. "It's started." He swung his arm in an enthusiastic if inaccurate punch.

Jerome prodded his wiimote politely back. His character made a half hearted wave in response.

"Oh, you need to give it more welly than that," said the PE teacher. "It's much more like real boxing than you think."

---

[68] Nintendo. (2008). "Wii." Retrieved 29th May, 2008, from http://www.nintendo.com/wii.

"Is that so?" said Jerome. "I used to box as an undergraduate." He shifted his weight forward onto his toes and punched the air a couple of times. "Now I feel it!"

"Nice one," said the teacher, with a new tone of respect.

"Oww!" said Jo. "You knocked me out!"

Ten minutes later Ada arrived at the stand to witness the unlikely spectacle of Jerome flattening Jo on screen, completely absorbed in the game. He was jumping, blocking, punching, dancing on his toes and breathing heavily.

"Hey, Ada," said Jo in relief. "Take over! Jerome's killing me!"

Ada laughed at him. "No way," she said. "I'll give you a game of *Guitar Hero*[69], though."

When the game finished, Jerome looked up and blinked a couple of times as if surprised to see the conference hall was still there. "I haven't boxed for years," he told the PE teacher, handing the wiimote back.

"You could teach my kids a thing or two," said the teacher. "They love these games. Same with the dance mats. It beats running round the playing fields in the mud, anyhow."

"You use this in your lessons?" queried Jerome.

"Often, yes. It's good for motivating the kids. Some of them don't like exercise but are willing to play games. It's a way to hook them in. They'll play *Wii Tennis* for ages, for example, and then they exercise for their 30 minutes a day without even noticing. One of my classes loves to use the dance mats. They get quite competitive. We had a university student come once who had programmed a new fitness game using the dance mat. It was like a

---

[69] Activision. (2008). "Guitar Hero." Retrieved 29th May, 2008, from http://www.guitarhero.com/.

Physical interfaces

mini Olympics with lots of different sports. My pupils tested it for him." [70]

"Fascinating," said Jerome. "Do you think it goes beyond simple motivation? I mean, do you think they gain fitness?"

"I do. We sometimes try them with heart rate monitors and next term I want to teach them how to do fitness tests so we can check their progress. I read an article once about a physiologist—his name was Dr Thin, believe it or not—who tested out some games like this in a lab to see if they made a difference to fitness. It turned out that yes, it did." [71]

Another teacher climbed onto the stand, carrying two cups of coffee. "We've got some *Guitar Hero* customers, I see. Here—have this one," he said handing over the coffee to his colleague. "I'm Derek," he said, turning to Jerome. "Are these your pupils?" he asked, pointing to Ada and Jo who were entering into the spirit of the game. Ada was dancing and swaying as she strummed her guitar and sang along to the music. Jo was jumping and banging his head in time.

"No, no," said Jerome, amused. "Ada's a bit old for that. But tell me, how does this game work?"

"You pick a song and a character. Once the concert starts the game shows you which chords to play, and you press the buttons on your guitar for the right chord. A lot of it's about rhythm but the game helps you by showing you on screen which chords are coming up and when to press them. Once you get good at it you

---

[70] For a similar game see Lewis Watson's free FitArcade game:Watson, L. (2007). "Fitarcade: An Exercise Game for Kids." Retrieved 29th May, 2008, from http://www.macs.hw.ac.uk/~judy/lww/www/game/index.htm.
[71] Thin, A. (2008). "GamerSize Science- Quest for the Perfect Exergame." Retrieved 29th May, 2008, from http://www.gamersizescience.org/.

start to hear for yourself when the chord is wrong, or when you play it at the wrong time."

"It is really like a guitar?" asked Jerome.

"No, not exactly but it means the pupils don't need to worry about what their fingers are doing. It makes one aspect of playing easier so they can focus on the whole experience of what it would be like to play at a concert. They get really into it. My class did a whole project around it where they formed a band, and they made lots of advertising material and studied geography to know where would be good tour venues. They wrote reviews for each other."[72]

"That's marvellous," said Jerome.

Jo, having defeated Ada convincingly, drifted off to play other games against the music and PE teachers. Ada joined Jerome.

"What do you reckon Jerome?" she asked. "More demon technology?"

"Not at all," said Jerome with dignity. "But I was wondering if there were any other examples where this sort of whole body interaction is used."

"Mmm," said Ada. "It's an emerging technology, but I think it will have a huge impact on technology design in general. The Wii is marketed at the whole family. You see all these pictures of old guys like you... I mean families playing together. It's a device to get games into the mainstream because you don't need to be able to use a computer to enjoy it. I would guess that other devices will follow, and more and more applications will be developed for the Wii, or using the wiimote. You can hook up the wiimote to a

---

[72]Derek Robertson did this work at Learning and Teaching Scotland. See *Blane, D. (2008). Creativity enters a new level. <u>Times Educational Supplement (Scotland)</u>. London: 12-13.*.

normal computer, as it happens. I have a student who is making a kids' drawing tool using the Wiimote instead of a mouse [73]."

"What's it like?" asked Chris who had brought Alex along to join in with Jo's game.

"Here," said Ada. "Watch the video." She handed Chris her phone and Jerome watched over her shoulder. "You use the wiimote and make gestures in the air. That draws on the canvas on screen. And different movements make different effects. Like you can delete it by making a cross in the air. Or you can make bubbles and have them follow your hand movements in the air"

"How lovely," said Chris. "It's just as if you were casting a magic spell."

"It's a nice example of what you would do with the Wii," admitted Ada. "With the drawing program it's a good half way house between the naturalness of ordinary drawing and the cool effects you can get when you digital drawing."

"I know younger children have trouble using the mouse for drawing at first," said Chris.

"Have you done any field studies of how it compares to pen and paper?" asked Jerome.

"Not yet," said Ada. "That's your job. Mine is to try this stuff out and see what we can do with it. But Jerome, use your imagination. Can't you see the possibilities?"

Jerome smiled at her "I can," he said. "I've never seen anything quite like this."

---

[73] For one example, see Robertson, J. (2007). "Student's video of a wii drawing tool." Retrieved 29th May, 2008, from http://judyrobertson.typepad.com/judy_robertson/2008/01/students-video.html. This is likely to be a popular project topic at lots of universities!

Inside Stories: A Narrative Journey

"I would love it if the children could make stories with it," said Chris. "Can you get a program for that, Ada?"

"At the moment it's so new, that it's a case of writing a program for that!" said Ada. "But I bet people will start to make apps like that. Actually, I have a friend who had a 'magic mirror' project[74] where kids could make stories by acting out scenes in front of a screen. They could see the character on screen making their movements. It's kind of like dressing up digitally. And they could have little props to use which looked different on screen. I wish they had that when I did drama at school."

"How curious," remarked Jerome. "It sounds a bit like playing with puppets."

"Kind of," said Ada. "Except you see the puppets make the same movement as you in a made-up world. Usually when you play with puppets you see your real self with the puppet on the end of your arm. Plus you can record your scene and show it to other people. Or you could change what your puppet looks like after you've recorded it if you change your mind."

"You're right, Ada," said Jerome. "There are possibilities there which I have never previously considered. We need to develop some further theory around these embodiment issues." [75]

"Yeah," said Ada. "People have done some of that theory stuff. Not quite my thing, though. Oh yeah, and there's tangible

---

[74] Good, J., Romero, P., du Boulay, B., Reid, H., Howland, K. and Robertson, J. (2008). An embodied interface for computational thinking. Intelligent User Interfaces, Canary Islands, Spain. Available from http://www.cogs.susx.ac.uk/users/bend/papers/iui08.pdf

[75] Jerome could start here: Dourish, P. (2001). Where the action is : the foundations of embodied interaction. Cambridge, Mass., MIT Press.

technology too, now I think of it. You know, with augmented reality." She broke off, seeing Chris's blank look.

"It's where you combine real live objects with digital technology. Usually you use RFID tags or bar codes, or image recognition through web cams. Imagine you had a toy farm with lots of little wooden animals. You could put a tiny RFID tag on each one and then the computer would know where each animal was placed in the toy farm yard. You could have a 3D farmyard on the computer screen with virtual versions of the same animals and when the kids moved the wooden pig over a scanner, then the computer could tell you information about the pig, or make a piggy noise or something. Actually, there've been various storytelling projects which are similar to that.[76]"

"What are RFID tags?" asked Chris.

"Those white stickers you get on the back on CDs when you buy them are RFID tags. They're quite small and cheap. The point of them is that you can use them to tell the computer which real world object you are interested in."

"Would it work it my children made little plasticine models of farm animals themselves and then put an RFID sticker on each one?" Chris wanted to know

"Hey- that's not a bad idea!" said Ada. "I don't see why not."

"It would certainly be more in line with a constructionist tradition," said Jerome. "The children could make their own contributions to the emerging story."

---

[76] Jim, B., M. Krystina, et al. (2007). PageCraft: learning in context a tangible interactive storytelling platform to support early narrative development for young children. <u>Proceedings of the 6th international conference on Interaction design and children</u>. Aalborg, Denmark, ACM.

Inside Stories: A Narrative Journey

"Maybe one of my students could do a project with your class," said Ada to Chris. "It would be fun to try that out."

Chris smiled. "I would love to," she said. "You know, all of these gadgets we've been looking at today could be important for storytelling. Alex and I were trying out games where you play bongo drums [77], and Jo and Ada were dancing. Normally I don't like computers much because it seems like your body gets left behind. You're like a brain in a vat. But with this sort of game your body and your mind are both involved. It's the same with stories. Often when I tell stories to younger children we have actions for them to join in with, or little rhymes which link the words to the movements to help them remember what happens. The gestures and movements I make put across the meaning of the story. If you add music or song to the story it adds a whole layer of meaning. "

"I suppose now we have these new interface devices then we could bring storytelling with the computer closer to real life storytelling," said Ada. "You could do extra things too, things you couldn't do with real life storytelling. You could tell stories which took place partly in your imagination and partly in a virtual world."

"That's true," said Chris. "But there are times when all you need is the story, the teller and the listener."

"It depends on the story," said Jerome. "Stories work well when you involve the mind and the body, for sure. Ada is suggesting intriguing new ways for doing this with these innovative technologies. But we also need to think about its

---

[77] Wikipedia, c. (4 May 2008 21:45 UTC). "Donkey Konga." Retrieved 29 May 2008 17:08 UTC, from
http://en.wikipedia.org/w/index.php?title=Donkey_Konga&oldid=210187041.

emotional resonance. Whether the story is told by a human helped along by technology, it should touch our hearts and tell us something about what it means to be human."

Goodbyes

Ada popped her head round the door of the speakers' room. "Do you have a moment, Jerome? I just want to say goodbye."

"Oh," Jerome said "You'll not stay for my talk?"

"Of course I will," Ada said. "I'll be your tech on call, as I promised. But I have to leave right after."

She held out her hand. "It was really nice to meet you. We had some interesting discussions."

Jerome said "Thank you Ada, I learned a lot about technology from you. And I will be in touch in time, I am sure, to find out more."

Ada said "Well remember I'll only answer emails or texts—no long letters written in your fountain pen!"

Jerome laughed. "Ok, Ada," he said, "I'll try it out again for your sake."

She put on one of her rare smiles and slid out of the door, putting in her ear phones as she went.

She hunted for Jo in the exhibition. As she expected, he was at the Wii stand. "Still rubbish, I see," she said, coming up right behind him.

"Oh! Ada," said Jo. "What do you want?"

"I just had to see you getting slaughtered on that thing once more before I leave," said Ada.

Jo grinned. "You're off then? Thank God for that."

"Take care," she said. "And hey—if you're on *World of Warcraft*, look me up. I'm Melinda Starflower"

"What kind of a name is that?" scoffed Jo. He unravelled from the Wii. "Hey, have you seen Jerome? I want to see him before his talk."

"In the speakers' room," said Ada. "Over there." She pointed. "See you, kid."

Jo headed over to the back of the exhibition suite where the speakers' room was. He found Jerome trying to write down the contents of his slides on a piece of paper.

"Jerome," said Jo sternly. "Didn't you promise Ada not to use paper for your presentation?"

Jerome looked up guiltily. "You won't tell, will you? Anyway I won't use it for the presentation. It's just in case the slides fail."

Jo made a face. "You know the slides won't fail really. Good luck anyway." He looked down at his shoes. "Jerome?"

"Yes?"

"You know before when you told me about the monkeys?"

"Yes."

"Well thanks. It was nice of you. I mean, I don't know if I really have monkeys in there, but it helped me to think about it."

"That's good," Jerome said. "I'm sure you will find a way to enjoy reading after all. And I will look out for your name on the next big animated film."

Jo grinned. "Yeah!" he said. "You just wait!"

Goodbyes

Peter saw Chris come out from the speakers' room. "How's Jerome?" he said "Is he very nervous?"

"He's fine," Chris said. "I'm much more nervous about it than he is."

Peter said "Don't worry, he'll do fine. And your class exhibition will be grand too. It's not until tomorrow anyway. How would you like to join me for dinner tonight after Jerome's talk?"

She looked at him.

"Errr. We could rehearse your exhibition?" he said hopefully.

"OK," said Chris, "I suppose I could do that. For the sake of the exhibition." But she smiled at him and he felt a glimmer of hope.

Ada, passing on her way to the coke machine, caught Chris' eye and grinned. "Way to go, Chris!" she said.

Chris glared at her but then softened into a reluctant smile. "It was really nice to meet you, Ada" she said, giving her a hug. "I hope you do come and visit my class sometime."

Ada gave her a bear hug. "You too. Give my love to monkey girl!"

Alex was in the speakers' room drawing mermaids on the mirror with Chris' lipstick. "What are you *doing*?" yelled Chris. "Honestly, I leave you for two minutes and you get yourself into trouble. Stop that!"

"Well, you were busy with Peter," said Alex slyly.

Chris changed the subject quickly. "Where did Jerome go?" she asked.

"He said he would be back in a minute" Alex answered.

"Well he better be because his talk is in 15 minutes, and he still has to get ready!"

She picked up his tweed jacket and brushed some hairs from it.

Jerome appeared in the doorway. "Oh thank you, Chris. You needn't do that."

Alex rushed at Jerome and threw her arms around his neck. "Good luck!" she said. "I bet everyone claps like mad"

Jerome smiled and patted her back. "They will when they see how good your drawings are," he told her. "I will miss you and all your stories, Alex. And you too Chris."

"It's OK," said Alex, "I will send you lots of letters and I could write a story for you every week in case you get all boring again without me."

Chris looked apologetically at Jerome, but having spent days in a train with Alex, he had grown a thick skin.

"As you will hear in my talk, I owe you so much from our discussions in the past days."

"Really?" asked Chris, "Do you mean it?"

He smiled at her. "I do. I hope one day I can come and visit your class and meet all your pupils. They are very lucky you know."

"Lucky?" said Alex. "Why?"

"Even if they don't know it," Jerome added.

Jerome's bag is returned

Chris was in the middle of straightening Jerome's bow tie, when there was a knock at the speakers' room door. She rushed to open it and was rather surprised to see the woman from The Medieval Tale stand at the fair, still wearing her medieval costume.

Jerome saw her reflection in the mirror and instantly turned towards her.

"Hilda!" he exclaimed, "Is that you?"

She blushed. "I've come with your brief case, Jerome. You left it my display in Hilarion and I heard in the news that you were to give a key note talk at the conference. So I thought you might need it."

Chris glanced from one to the other. "Did you really come all this way to give him his briefcase? That's really sweet".

Jerome hurried across the room and politely ushered her into a chair. "Thank you *so* much. How very considerate. Please, do have something to drink."

Chris said "You're just in time to hear Jerome's talk, Hilda." She stopped. "But which version of the talk are you going to give?"

Jerome paused as he poured Hilda's juice. "My goodness. My old talk. It's still there. But should I use it? I don't know…"

Chris stepped in to mop up the orange juice that was pouring over the side of the glass. "Pay attention, Jerome," she said. "Well, I suppose you have a choice now. What are you going to do?"

Jerome pondered as he walked back and forth, obviously agitated by this last minute challenge. On the one hand, in his brief case, he had his carefully prepared handwritten manuscript, in his familiar fluent handwriting in his favourite pen. And then there was the laptop Ada was setting up in the room next door. He felt in his pocket for the laser pointer she had taught him to use. He thought about Chris, who had helped him with his story, and of Ada and Peter who had patiently helped him with the slides. He thought how disappointed Alex and Jo would be if he didn't use their art work. And he thought of all he had learned in the last few days. Suddenly the decision was not hard to make. "Of course I will give the presentation that we have prepared together," he said. "I have no second thoughts about that."

Chris glanced at her watch. "You're on, Jerome," she said.

Jerome took Hilda's hand briefly. "Thank you so much for coming all this way," he said. "After the talk would you like to have a drink with me?"

"Yes," said Hilda. "I would like that."

The Future of Narrative and Learning Technology

The loudspeaker in the great conference hall announced. "We now present the closing key-note with Jerome Fletcher from the Learning Theory Centre in Brussels who has been gracious enough to come here as a Professor Emeritus and present his thoughts on the future of narrative and learning technology".

Jerome stepped onto the platform. Ada had previously loaded up his slides and they were ready to use at the click of a button. He opened his first slide, adjusted his bow tie and beamed at the audience.

The Future of Narrative and Learning Technology

"Thank you for inviting me here today. From the title of my talk you already know that I will be talking on narrative and the future of learning. As you all know, narrative is an old and fundamental way of making sense of things. My colleague Dr. Sarbin has put it very clearly when he first proposed the existence of a narrative principle:

'I propose the narratory principle: that human beings think, perceive, imagine and make moral choices according to narrative structures. Present two or three pictures, or descriptive phrases, to a person and he or she will connect them to form a story, an account that relates the pictures or the meaning of the phrases in some patterned way.'[78]

"This principle is in line with research on perceived causality done by Michotte[79]. He was interested in how the movement of geometrical figures was perceived as causally related and one figure was either seen as dragging the other or being pushed. Similar experiments were done by the psychologists Fritz Heider and Marianne Simmel[80]. Using a film with geometrical figures of two triangles, a circle and a rectangle moving around, they demonstrated how practically all their informants experienced an intention behind the movements of the figures, and they became actors in a story. I have the film here."

---

[78] Sarbin, T. R. (1986). Narrative psychology : the storied nature of human conduct. New York, Praeger.

[79] Michotte, A. E. d., E. Miles, et al. (1963). The Perception of Causality. (Translation by T. R. Miles and Elaine Miles.), pp. xxii. 425. Methuen & Co.: London.
[80] Heider, F. a. S., M. (1944). "An Experimental Study of Apparent Behavior " The American Journal of Psychology 57(2): 243-259.

Inside Stories: A Narrative Journey

Very carefully, Jerome navigated to his desktop and double clicked on the file which Peter had prepared for him. A video started playing.

"Hmm. He's moved into the 21st century since I last saw him," muttered an audience member to her neighbour.

"Shhh," she replied. "This is really interesting. Jerome knows his narrative theory better than anyone."

"The film illustrates our propensity to see stories from the simplest of shapes. Storytelling is an important part of our experience, and can play an important part in learning. We must now consider what part it may play in the future of learning, and the role technology may play also.

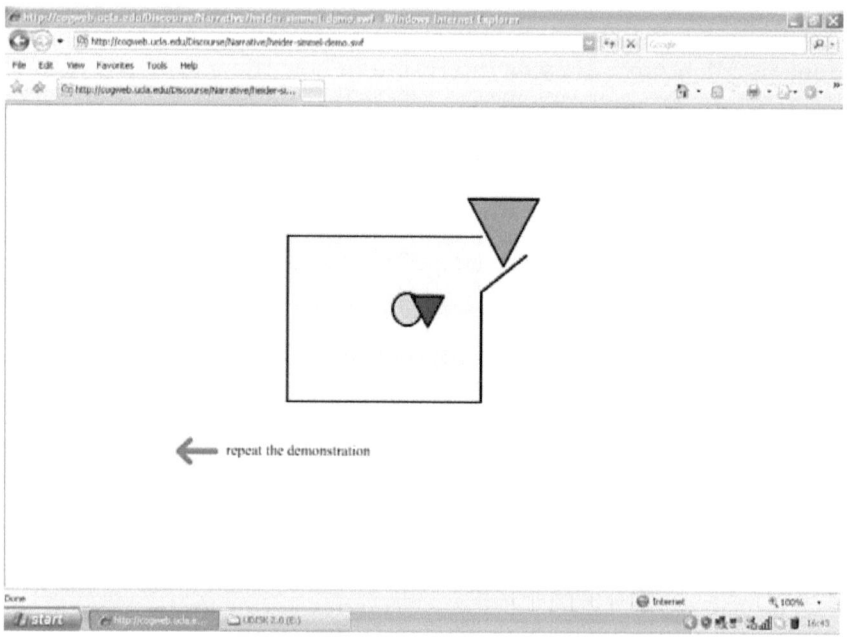

The video Jerome showed of Heider and Simmel's work

"When I started out on this journey, I came filled with all the things I already knew. I thought that technology was much

The Future of Narrative and Learning Technology

overrated, was a foreign element in the classroom, difficult to master, and disruptive for the communication between teacher and learner. I came here to show that—as in the tale of the Emperor's New Clothes, when the truth was revealed by a small child—it would come nothing. I was convinced that there was not really anything in this, except a distraction to both teacher and learner.

"'What is the meaning of technology?' one may ask. Is it not true that every new technology is costly, time consuming to learn, and ultimately may deter us from focusing on developing the skills of good teaching, of getting to know each other better? Is in not true that technology is for doing things more effectively and rapidly but in a superficial way? I've looked at countless e-learning systems; I was part of committee looking at e-learning and I was appalled. It was boring, lifeless and bureaucratic."

A couple of participants who had wisely placed themselves close to the exit at the end of the row of seats demonstratively yawned. One whispered to the other, "There he goes again. He'll never see the light."

"As you may know, I resigned from this committee, but not because I was opposed to using technology as such. Rather what I saw seemed like a dead-lock, keeping the learners in a situation akin to the worst of distance education, not something I would think was the solution to bringing education to the world.

"A different approach is needed—but what? Not necessarily a narrative approach, but one that takes this into account. Narrative is such a fundamental state of mind, of expression and of comprehension, it would not be fruitful to design the learning environments for the future without taking narrative into account.

Inside Stories: A Narrative Journey

"I was surprised when you asked me to give the key-note, but today I'm glad that you did. On my journey here and in these days I've seen some glimpses of how technology may actually enrich the learning experience. So I have a story to tell you here today—my young friend Alex asked me to put a story into my talk. This is for her, but it makes a serious point. As you know, stories are about transformations. Some of you may be surprised to see what happened to an old researcher who has always treasured the book.

"An old man walked through the snow. All throughout his life he had been travelling through the country searching for knowledge. When he visited new towns and villages he would stop and talk to people, and ask them to tell him things he did not know. Often they would bring him their most treasured books to read. He carried a sack with him, and when he heard something new or interesting he would put it in his sack. Now he was nearing the end of his life, he often worried what would become of his sack—who would care for his knowledge when he was gone? This particular night was cold and he hurried along as best he could to try to find a warm house. The sack of knowledge grew heavier with every step. The nearest building he came to was made from black glass and it towered above the surrounding town. A woman in a silver dress greeted him at the door. 'I'm looking for knowledge. And some food and warmth,' he said. 'Come in old man,' she said. 'Here you can find all the knowledge in the world at the snap of my fingers.' The room he entered was large with a glass vaulted ceiling. The sorceress, for that was who she was, fetched him some food and drink. As he ate, she spoke of the riches of knowledge that she could give him. He was entranced, but wary. She asked him about his sack and he explained that it was his collection of knowledge

The Future of Narrative and Learning Technology

gathered over all the years of his life. 'And now I must find someone else to continue my work.' 'Perhaps,' said the sorceress, with a mysterious smile, 'Perhaps.'

That night the old man slept under the glass ceiling, with his sack clutched to his chest as always. In the small hours of the night, the sack started to move. The knowledge was restless. From the dark recesses of the room he could hear scrabbling and chirping. As the sounds came closer the sack started to jump more violently. The old man sat up to watch, and to his horror, he saw an army of small dark shapes advancing on him. Green, red and orange lights blinked somewhere in the darkness.

'Dragon flies? Glow-worms?' he wondered. But as they grew closer he became more and more frightened. This was something far worse.

He was soon surrounded by a crowd of devices: laptops, mobile phones, and PDAs. He shrank back in terror, trying to protect his precious sack of knowledge. But the knowledge itself wanted out. It scratched at the sack from the inside and the PDAs and mobiles nibbled at the sack from the outside. The laptops snapped their lids open and closed to tear the fabric. Very soon the sack burst open and a cloud of moths flew out, drawn towards the blinking lights.

'My knowledge!' moaned the old man in despair. Even as he watched the moths were fluttering higher and higher into the air until they left through the glass atrium.

The door opened and the sorceress entered. The devices turned and scuttled towards her, fawning at her silver robes affectionately. 'What is wrong?' she asked.

'The work of my life has come to nothing! Your creatures have opened my sack of knowledge and now it is dispersed. Lost.'

'Dispersed, yes. But nothing is lost.'

'Please help,' The old man asked. 'I cannot get all my knowledge back myself.'

'Of course I will help. We will all help.'

She snapped her fingers and her army of creatures marched into an orderly line. 'Go and find all the knowledge which was in that sack,' she instructed. 'Every last scrap of it. And quickly!'

Almost instantly the creatures left. And almost instantly they were back.

That which was lost returns

The old man moaned once more. 'I knew it. They couldn't find anything!'

'Of course they did,' she smiled. And she beckoned to the first of the laptops who came forward respectfully and opened its jaws. A beautiful butterfly fluttered out, unharmed by the gentle laptop.

The Future of Narrative and Learning Technology

The old man peered at it. It was a familiar friend—a scrap of knowledge he had gathered many years before, except that it had grown. It was both bigger and more beautiful than it had been before.

'What happened?' exclaimed the old man.

The sorceress looked at him. 'Your knowledge,' she said 'met the knowledge of the rest of the world. And see—it was transformed. But still you recognise it. And this is the answer to your question and to your search. You wanted to know who would care for your knowledge. The answer, you see, is everyone. Anyone who can share your knowledge can add to it, and share it with everyone else.'

The old man looked wonderingly at the devices which were now playfully chasing the thousands of butterflies which filled the room.

'I could not imagine how this could have been done before,' he said. 'It goes beyond anything one man could do himself.'

The sorceress looked proudly at her creatures. 'They cannot do this by themselves,' she said. 'They need people to direct them where to look. But used wisely, they can be a great help to us.'

The old man left the sorceress the next day, waving goodbye to all but one of the small creatures. The sorceress had chosen one of her favourite smart phones to accompany on his journey and send her some of the new knowledge he created. The creatures would store copies of everything in his sack to keep it safe. She told him that anytime he needed to find knowledge other people had created, his creature would bring it to him. He set out with a new spring in his step. The sack which had weighed him down for so many years felt as light as the air itself."

"Hey, that's like Jerome's dream," said Jo, surprised.

"But different," said Alex, "He changed it."

"What on earth was that about?" the man in the row in front of Chris asked. "Gentle laptops? How soppy can you get?"

"Talk about anthropomorphism!" agreed his colleague.

"Hmm. A new treatment of the journey tale," said the lady in the front row. "Unexpected for Jerome."

"How many of you could relate to the story?" Jerome asked, not really knowing what to expect. He looked surprised as a forest of hands quickly rose up in the air. Ada whistled loudly. "Go Jerome!" she yelled. Jerome continued after the audience settled down.

"Of course, that story has a moral in it, because I deliberately constructed it in that fashion. Some of you may agree with the sentiment, while others may be opposed. Some of you may spot problems with the analogy in the tale. Each of you will take something different from it. But the point I wanted to make was that we need to retain the connection to our roots, but explore the possibilities offered to us by new technology. We need to be able to let go of worn out ways of thinking but still keep a connection to that which has genuine value. This is what educational research should strive for.

"I can see many of the challenges that are meeting the learners of this millennium and of the future. One challenge is how to combine the potentials of technology with content that is both enriching and valuable for the learner."

Jerome advanced his slide to show the diagram he had prepared on the train, helped by Alex. The academics at the back peered at the diagram. "What on earth is that?" one asked. Alex tapped the one closest to her on the shoulder with sticky fingers," I helped draw it," she said proudly. Chris grabbed Alex's hand from the owner of corporate pin-striped suit. "Sorry"

He gave Alex a withering glance, and then he turned to his companion whispering, "This thing is becoming more and more of a circus."

Jerome went on to explain "You'll notice that in this diagram there is a central axis, which divides affect from cognition, and you'll see that this line is coiled across the boundaries of cognition and affect, between thought and feeling. By no means must you interpret this as a static model. It fluctuates between internal and external, and between affect and cognition.

"This axis runs between the two dimensions of internal and external construction of story. The top half of the diagram is the individual area where the learner is making meaning at a personal level, drawing on his or her individuality, her own personal history and all other stories that she has ever heard. In this case imagine a listener who hears a story told by another and imagines this story world inside her head.

"This meaning making is happening on a cognitive level through making sense of the structure, understanding causal relations and making inferences. On the affective level the meaning making includes empathizing with emotional impact of the story, and identifying with characters and immersing oneself in the story-world.

"At the other end of this line, in the external direction, you find the social dimension where stories have a cultural value and resonance. Stories exist to be told and by expressing them the learner becomes part of the culture. This process of articulation is also important to the sense of identity, and some stories are understood by being articulated. Here we have story-making as a cognitive tool. The construction of story is a cognitive as well as affective process. We are talking about learners making up new stories, or sharing stories they have heard with other people. The point is that the events are no longer imagined in the learner's head: he must find words to explain his meaning to his listeners."

Jerome paused and stared at the audience. The audience stared back, puzzled.

"OK ," he said, "This will become clearer with an example. My good friend, Chris, told us the story of the *Paper Bag Princess* during the journey. In the story there is a fantasy *setting* which contains princesses, dragons and castles. There is a *situation* in which a princess is able to rescue a prince. And we have of course the *characters*: the paper bag princess, the handsome prince Ronald, and the stout Mr. Dragon.

"While listening to this story, the listener begins to use the cognitive skill of analogy to map between the setting, the situation of the story to similar environments and issues within real life.

"In some stories there is such emotional impact that the listener cannot help but to feel what the character feels. You all know this, if you have watched a film that is so sad that you leave the cinema with tears rolling down your cheeks. This of course relates to affective development. In other cases one might experience cognitive empathy. For example you might think 'If I were the paper bag princess I would not bother rescuing Prince Ronald.' This is empathy at a distance: understanding the feeling of a character, but being able to reason about what the character could and should do next.

The Future of Narrative and Learning Technology

"This process between mapping between story and real life is necessary for narrative learning. Think of it as understanding the moral of the story and how it relates to your own life, such that you may change your own behaviour in the future. And so by listening to the story of the courageous Paper Bag Princess, young Alex can learn that in the future she too can overcome the challenges of gender stereotypes. I hope that she grows up with such a bold and fearless outlook as part of her identity."

Ada was surprised. She had never thought of Jerome as that much of a feminist. Alex looked solemnly at Jerome with round eyes. Chris squeezed her shoulder. "I'll try," said Alex to Chris, "I'll really try."

"Now I'll like to give an example to illustrate the external direction of the axis. During the journey I was privileged to meet a dedicated and conscientious and yes—*inspiring* teacher. She told me about her classes work on sea-life stories."

Chris blinked rapidly and Ada nudged her in the ribs.

"In the sea-life project, the children first listened to stories about the sea. They also learned through direct experiences of visiting the seaside and researching the sorts of creatures that you find there. Then they started to make their own stories to share with one another, and in doing so they were sharing their different understandings and interests. They were exercising their cognitive skills of creating a story within a coherent and internally consistent framework."

"The line coils into affect at this end of the axis," said Jerome, making an expansive sweeping gesture with his hand.

"In order for the children to create stories that are compelling to the other children they must enter the affective realm, they must imagine how their characters will feel and behave. And their actions are often based on their feelings and interpretations of other characters' feelings. You could say that they are practicing emotional gymnastics and this requires on the cognitive side some theories of mind.

"I spoke before about how you may make an analogy between a story and your life. In this case there may be a mapping between the children's lives and the stories they choose to create. It may be that the stories they tell are a projection of their identity or an aspect of their identity. But this may not be conscious on the part of the child. This leads me to consider the role of teachers in supporting children in meaning making through stories. While children develop narrative skills in early childhood, this skill is developed through interactions with parents, with brothers and sisters, and peers in the Vygotskian process with which most of you may be familiar."

The pin-striped suit raised his hand. "Vygotsky?" he asked, "I'm sorry but I'm not familiar with this software."

Jerome looked scandalized. "Young man," he said, "I speak of Vygotsky, the early 20th century psychologist who is renowned for his contribution to developmental psychology. I was referring to his so-called zone of proximal development, where he points to the role a more able partner can play in helping you extend your capabilities. For example, a mother may coax a more elaborated story by asking questions when her child describes her day at school."

The pin-striped suit was obviously embarrassed; maybe that was what his academic collaborators had been trying to get across at the last project meeting.

The Future of Narrative and Learning Technology

"Much research has already been done on narrative structures and their development in children in various ages. These are present in various degrees of sophistication from an early age. By listening to stories and telling stories children are practicing these meaning making capabilities. The interesting thing is that when you add a meta-cognitive level and start to make the story structures obvious and transparent by actually analyzing stories in their narrative components, the children quickly improve their external story-making skills. A good teacher can do this and also help the children with the analogical mapping between the story-world and their own world."

Alex got restless. "Ana—what?" she whispered, "You've not been helping me with those Ana whats its."

"Analogies," said Chris. "Shhhh. I'll tell you later."

"You might be wondering," continued Jerome, "about what all this has to do with technology."

"Too right," muttered the pin-striped suit.

"I would argue," said Jerome, "and this is an argument that I have not made before, that technology can also assist in scaffolding children as story-makers. We know in school classes how challenging it can be for the teacher to be there for all of the children. Often there are slow learners that need more assistance, but then the quicker learners get bored. The ideal is of course to provide the right level of challenge and stimulation for all of the children. From what I have seen and heard the last days it is obvious that technology can have a very important role in assisting the teacher in creating an environment where learners can learn and express at their own pace. It can also have an important role to play in opening up fictional worlds for children to experience.

"The important thing in coming to understand the potential of technology in the classroom is to view it as a *tool*. Teachers use tools all the time in the class. They find new purposes for poor tools and exploit the advantages of good tools. They are infinitely inventive, when it comes to finding good uses for the tools they find around them.

"Tools are important in education," Jerome swept on. "Tools change things. Technology is a tool to think with and a tool to feel with, it is tool to share with and a tool to imagine with. If you look at this model, you'll find four areas." He advanced his slide and pointed to the highlighted area in the top left space.

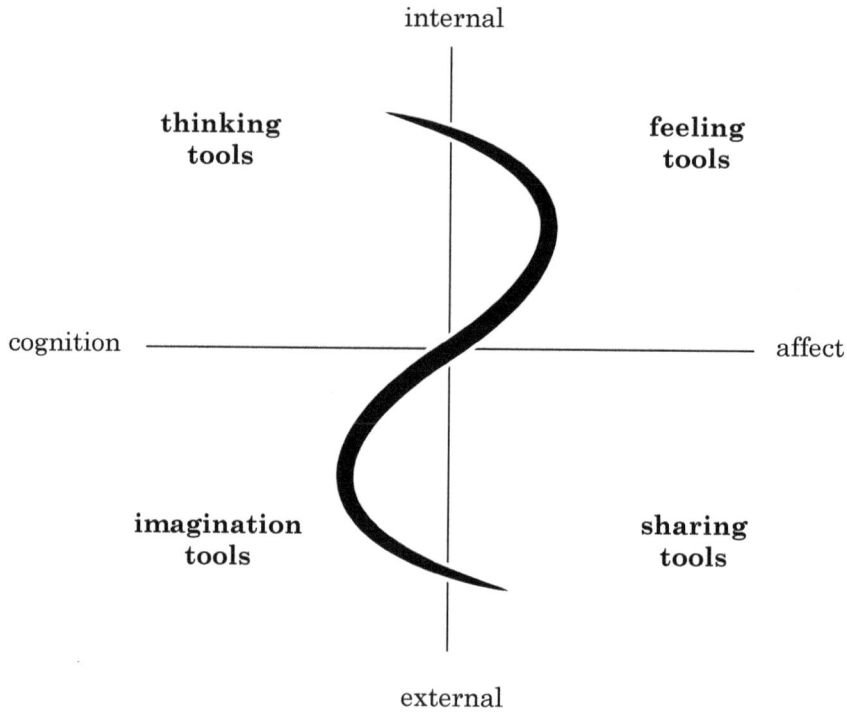

Jerome's diagram, showing how technology tools can support narrative.

Seymour Papert of course, gave us the idea of technology as a tool to *think* with. We know that technology can help us to think by saving us effort, by reducing our cognitive load through external representations. It can also give us a simulation in which to pursue the answers to 'what if' questions. For example, an interactive multimedia story, perhaps in the form of a game, supports learners in meaning making by challenging them to consider the multiple meanings and perspective in the story because it enables them to repeatedly explore different paths of a story in sequence.

"In the bottom left corner," he said circling it with his mouse pointer, "the external cognition can be supported if you consider technology as a tool to *imagine* with. By which I mean, that children who have not developed their imagination or language can be greatly helped if they are provided with artefacts they can choose between when constructing a story. The story elements are represented externally, and the learners through building stories out of the artefacts, can develop narrative competencies that they would not develop otherwise. It is a way of scaffolding learners on the way to free-form imaginative creations. Further, some forms of creative products cannot be made in any other medium such as games.

"In the bottom right quadrant, technology can be tool to *share* with. Sharing is an important element of externalization from an affective point of view because learners get much satisfaction and pleasure from having others review their work. A story is lost without an audience, and technology simply makes it easier to quicker to share a story with others. This may be an audience that the learner would never normally reach—for example in the conference you can see posters about projects where Australian children commented on the stories produced by their pen pals in Scotland. I have learned about the power of social networking during my journey. I believe that there are important parallels between storytelling and social networking. With both, people are driven to share their thoughts with others and are eager to get feedback from their audience."

He pointed to the fourth and last quadrant in the diagram. "It is less common to talk about technology as a tool to *invoke feeling*. In fact I would never have considered this until I met my companions on this train journey. Let us consider how technology may support internal affect. Or even, how technology may *invoke* internal affect. I learned on this trip of software called *Fear Not!* which is designed to help children deal with issues relating to bullying. The children can empathise with the characters in the scenarios and offer them advice. This gives them a way to test out the efficacy of their advice in a safe way. Another project called *Working Things Out* has been used in a therapy setting. It is a series of animations created by young people with emotional difficulties about their experiences. It can be used to assist other young people by showing them that they are not alone in the feelings that they have. The young people who created the animations were using technology both to express their feelings and share them. The young people who viewed the animations could use them to reason about what they might do it in similar situations.

"Of course effective narrative learning can be achieved without technology. But equally there are some situations where the technology enables something which would not previously have been possible. Let me illustrate this with an example from a well designed narrative learning environment. On the journey here I met a teacher who showed software called *A Medieval Tale*."

The Future of Narrative and Learning Technology

Jerome switched the slide to show a collage of screenshots and photographs which Jo had helped him to create. "This software is designed to help children with multiple functional deficits to experience stories. It supports learners in different aspects of the narrative model. For example the learners can watch stories with their teacher and classmates and switching into external affect they can show the teacher and class-mates preferences they cannot express verbally by making choices with the software. In this case the software supports both external cognition and affect, and the software is a powerful enabler. Now with this particular group of learners, it is difficult for the teachers to understand what happens internally, because the learners are often unable to express it. However in the internal affective space, *A Medieval Tale* is designed to encourage the children to empathize and identify with the story characters."

Jerome glanced at the clock.

"In this talk, I have described my own journey to understanding the relationship new technologies can have with narrative learning. I have presented a model of narrative learning which emphasizes the dynamic and fluctuating process which moves between cognition and affect, and the cyclical process constantly moving between internal meaning making and external sharing of meaning. Of course, others before me have presented models of narrative and learning because it is of such fundamental importance. The focus of the model I have presented here today is the interplay between affect and cognition, and internal and external representations. It is simply a view point on the topic which I hope you will find useful. I have discussed some examples of how technology can be used to support learning within this model, and how in some cases, technology enables learning to happen in a new way which would not have previously been possible. At the exhibition we will all see wonderful examples of innovative technologies. If you use your imagination you will see that there are great possibilities for storytelling here. For example you could tell stories which take place partly in your imagination and partly in a virtual world. But you must also stop and think—what is the best way to tell the story you wish to express? "Sometimes the story only needs a teller and a listener. Other times you may wish to allow technology to take you to previously uncharted story worlds. The main point to remember is that the content of the story itself is important, just as the relevance and quality of any educational material should be our priority. It should feed the imagination as well of the mind of the learners. Therefore you must consider whether the story really touches the heart. Regardless of whether the story is told by a human storyteller or mediated by technology, it should touch our hearts and engage our minds. It should tell us something about what it means to be human."

Index

A Medieval Tale, 178, 179, 180, 183, 187, 286
affect, 244, 245, 246, 279, 281, 286, 287
animation, 31, 71, 72, 94, 225, 226, 227, 245
assessment, 99, 104, 105
augmented reality, 132, 263
authentic learning, 73, 78
blogs, 223, 224, 225, 226, 227, 228
bullying, 14, 139, 200, 201, 202, 203, 205, 207, 208, 209, 210, 211, 286
classroom projects, 65, 69
cognition, 34, 35, 141, 217, 242, 244, 245, 279, 280, 281, 282, 283, 285, 287
cognitive load, 34, 35, 285
comics, 25, 189, 190, 195, 208
confidence building, 32
curriculum areas, 67
Curriculum for Excellence, 194
drama, 14, 68, 71, 167, 202, 204, 219, 221, 246, 262

realism, 167
dyslexia, 22, 67, 93, 94, 95
Ecolab, 135, 136
evaluation methods, 108
example stories
  Godmother Death, 112
  The Girl Who Married a Lion, 52
  The Grasshopper and the Ant, 44
  The Grasshopper and the Ant, Version 2, 45
  The Paper Bag Princess, 85
  The Raven Brothers, 89
  The Spider in the Yucca, 23
exclusion, 176
experiential learning, 61, 73
facts, 46, 47, 65, 66, 254
  distinguishing from stories, 47
FearNot, 202, 204, 205, 206, 207, 240
female role-models, 92
frame story, 35, 185
games
  balancing, 160
  game authoring, 168

hypothesis testing, 151
hypothesis testing, 150
physical, 256, 257, 258, 259, 260, 265, 266
violence, 209
gender, 200
gender differences, 50
GPS, 137
imaginary friends, 139
imagination, 32, 94, 138, 139, 140, 141, 238, 261, 264, 285, 288
learning
  authentic, 73
  experiential, 73
Lego, 222, 223
listening, 67, 68, 96, 101, 103, 104, 280, 281, 283
literacy
  media, 254
  written, 67
Literacy, media, 254
massively multiplayer online games, 212, 214, 215, 216, 239
meta-narrative, 185
models, 14, 36, 86, 263, 287
modes of thought, 48, 66
moral messages, 58
moral value, 45, 46

multiple perspectives, 54, 57, 62
narrative
  cognition, 36
  learning, 241, 246, 281, 286, 287
  learning environment, 246, 286
  mode of thought, 50
  model, 287
  principle, 271
  structure, 271, 283
Neverwinter Nights, 145, 146, 165
personalisation, 144
personalised learning, 137
play, 141
reciprocal apprenticeship, 218
role-play, 62
Second Life, 213, 220, 221, 239
social networking, 224, 230, 245, 285
special needs, 180
story
  definition, 30
  Labov model, 36, 37
  repetition, 39
  types, 43

story drama, 219
story type
  beast epic, 41, 42
  etiological, 41, 91
  myth, 90, 214
storytelling
  emergent, 219
  in the classroom, 33
  oral, 38
  power of, 32, 67
  telephone, 139
  therapeutic, 116
successful learner skills, 194
tangible interfaces, 223, 262
technology
  facilitation, 193

problem solving, 193
tools
  feeling, 247
  imagination, 245, 285
  sharing, 245, 286
  technology, 284
  thinking, 244, 285
user generated content, 31, 46, 47, 49, 228, 250, 251, 253, 254, 255
violence, 25, 26, 116, 208, 209
Wikipedia, 256
World of Warcraft, 212, 213, 215, 266
writing for an audience, 227

www.ingramcontent.com/pod-product-compliance
Ingram Content Group UK Ltd.
Pitfield, Milton Keynes, MK11 3LW, UK
UKHW041258180426
11947UKWH00008B/545